ISBN 1-74123-010-1

PLAN AND MANAGE CONFERENCES

by

Beverley L. Weynton

Software Publications

PLAN AND MANAGE CONFERENCES

© Copyright Beverley L. Weynton, January 2003

Author: BEVERLEY L. WEYNTON

Editor: GREG TAYLOR

ISBN: 1-74123-010-1

Disclaimer

Publishers – Software Publications Pty Ltd (ABN 75 078 026 150)

Head Office – Sydney
Unit 10, 171 Gibbes Street
Chatswood NSW 2067
Australia

Web Address
www.softwarepublications.com

Branches

Adelaide, Brisbane, Melbourne, Perth and Auckland

PLAN AND MANAGE CONFERENCES

BSBADM 503A

Beverley Weynton

CONTENTS

1 Plan conferences

In this first element we examine the purposes, outcomes and styles of conferences, the different types of conference requirements and the time required to make preparations. This includes arranging speakers or presenters, preparing the conference program based on the elements it contains, and briefing the speakers.

Next, the target group expected to attend the conference is identified as well as the number of possible attendees.

Finally, the administration requirements for the management of the conference are considered, including efficient management of the data and resources that are available.

1.1 Purpose, outcomes and style confirmed with convener

Conferences can mean different things to different people or organisations, and there are many reasons or purposes for convening one. Conferences can range in duration from a single day to four or five days and may be *formal* or *informal* in style.

*To **confer** means to 'discuss or consult together'; to 'compare opinions.'*

*A **conference** is 'a meeting for formal consultation or discussion'; 'an official assembly'.*

***Informal** means 'relaxed and friendly', or 'not according to prescribed or customary forms'.*

***Formal** means 'following established conventions', 'methodical and organised.*

Formal conferences

A formal conference is likely to be conducted in a similar way to a board meeting, where some members of senior management or the directors of a company are seated at a table on a stage or dais with a chairperson conducting the meeting.

Concurrently means 'occurring side by side'; 'taking place at the same time'.

The purpose of this type of meeting is usually to discuss policies and obtain the views of attendees on certain subjects. There would be speakers on the various items under consideration, but their function would be to explain a proposed policy or subject and to answer questions on it, rather than offer opinions or relate personal experiences.

A **delegate** is 'a person chosen to represent others at a conference'.

A formal conference is more likely to have an agenda rather than a program, and all the sessions would be held in the same hall rather than be broken up into a range of different sessions, some running *concurrently*, in a series of smaller rooms, as sometimes occurs at less formal conferences.

Standing orders

There may be rules which govern formal conferences set down or incorporated in the standing orders of the organisation. This would mainly apply to companies that hold regular conferences. The rules would deal with the way motions were to be moved, how long a speaker may address the meeting and the chairperson's authority in conducting the conference.

If no standing orders apply, then the organising committee would need to set down rules for the conduct of the particular conference and these would be read out to the assembly at the opening session of the conference by the chairperson.

Formal conferences are usually attended by *delegates* representing each branch of an organisation, and are usually given the power to vote on behalf of their branches.

Other types of conferences

Some conferences—either formal or informal—can be arranged for purely commercial reasons, while others may focus on the professional development of a selected group of a company's staff. Others may be arranged *exclusively* for the members of an association with the main purpose of sharing information among a *peer group*.

Conferences are often convened for members of a particular organisation, profession or special interest group. If you worked in the field of architectural design, accountancy or science, for example, your professional association would probably arrange annual or *biennial* conferences for its members.

Attendees would be able to listen to invited speakers—some recognised experts in their field – discussing new techniques or ways of working, new products *pertinent* to the profession, or findings and developments resulting from research. Also, there may be opportunities for individuals to choose from different workshops, discussion groups or question-and-answer sessions to learn more about specific areas of interest within their profession, if provision for these has been made in the program.

Company conferences

Annual conferences may be convened by the CEO (Chief Executive Officer) or managing director of a company or business at which employees of middle management level and above would be expected to attend. The attendees could also include the company's sales force.

This type of conference would be conducted in a formal manner and is more likely to focus on new products or those in development, and to seek feedback from staff on the way the company is performing or is perceived to be performing. A review of the past year would be part of the agenda, and perhaps motivational speakers would be invited to lead some sessions. Other speakers would be team leaders or divisional heads reviewing the past 12 months' activities and achievements of their groups, with an *overview* of activities and goals planned for the coming year.

Other, less formal types of company conferences may take the form of a 'reward' to executives or key personnel for the previous year's hard work and achievements. The CEO may invite the board of directors and other selected staff members to take part in a conference at a resort such as an island on the Great Barrier Reef or some other exotic location. Whilst some serious formal discussions or meetings and

Exclusive means 'limited to designated objects (or people)'; 'shutting out all others'.

A **peer group** is 'a group of people of the same occupation'.

Biennial means every two years.

Pertinent means 'related to or connected with the matter in hand'.

An **overview** is a comprehensive survey.

strategic planning sessions would be scheduled, the main purpose would be bonding, sharing of ideas and relaxation.

Purposes and required outcomes for convening a conference

The most common purposes for convening a conference would include the following:

- marketing of new products;
- promoting a company or its products;
- expanding business contacts and networking;
- training staff;
- presenting and sharing research findings or other types of information;
- professional development;
- obtaining views of attendees on certain subjects;
- reviewing a company's overall performance and activities; and
- to bring together members and employees spread throughout the country or the world, or various combinations of the above.

Combination of outcomes and purposes

An example of a combination of purposes and outcomes of a conference could be an English Teachers' Association conference. While the majority of attendees would be members of the association (i.e. teachers from all over Australia and perhaps from overseas), editors and representatives from textbook and children's books publishers would also be present and attend some of the sessions.

Defray means to 'provide money to cover costs or expenses'.

As a part of the conference, and to help *defray* the costs of mounting it, publishers would be invited to display their products (for an agreed fee) and to act as sponsors for some aspects of it. For example, larger publishers may *underwrite* the cost of printing the conference program or the name tags for attendees, or provide the wine at the conference dinner, in exchange for greater *prominence* of their name at the conference.

To *underwrite* means to 'agree to give a certain sum of money'; 'to meet the expense of'.

A large area adjoining the conference rooms would be booked and allocated for publishers to set up stands to display and write orders for their publications and other educational materials, hand out catalogues or brochures and generally promote their company's

Prominence means 'standing out so as to be easily seen'; 'very noticeable, importance'.

products and authors. The revenue raised from payments for these display areas would help fund the conference so fees for delegates could be kept affordable.

Positive outcomes

Some of the positive required outcomes for publishers would be that their editors and sales staff would benefit from attending some sessions to learn about the latest findings in the teaching of English and other matters of professional interest. They may also be able to identify possible new authors for their company among the workshop leaders and speakers at the conference. The company's profile would be raised and its products would be promoted and sold and a large group of potential customers reached for a reasonable outlay of funds.

Sales representatives would have a stream of delegates visiting their stands, examining their products, ordering some, and seeking information about others over a period of several days. The sales representatives and the delegates would also be able to view and compare the other publishers' products in one place at the same time. Networking and exchanging information with other publishers, teachers and educational advisors could also lead to valuable outcomes for all concerned.

The positive outcomes or benefits for the Association, apart from arranging and conducting a successful conference, would be the financial support from the publishers that hired display areas or sponsored some aspects of the conference, allowing the association to break even or even have a modest surplus.

Organising an exhibition

If the conference committee considers that a trade display or exhibition would be an appropriate addition to the conference as an income-generating exercise as well as adding interest for conference delegates, potential exhibitors should be identified and approached. The list of possible exhibitors would comprise companies that would consider delegates to the conference as potential buyers of their products.

Fees

Sometimes different sizes of display areas are allocated for different fees. However, it is important that the fees charged will cover the hire of the exhibition space as well as any setting up required, while allowing a small profit for the company or association.

Confirming display area

Once an exhibitor has booked and paid for a display area, a space should be allocated and marked on the floor plan of the exhibition area and a letter of confirmation sent to the exhibitor with a receipt for the fee paid.

Details such as whether tables and chairs will be available, the location and identifying number of the display stand, power points and setting up and dismantling times should be included. Information about where representatives may park to unload display materials would be helpful, as would a map of these areas.

The letter should also set out information about the conference including the beginning and closing times each day and the break times for morning and afternoon tea and lunchtime. These will be the busiest times for the exhibitors.

Health and safety requirements

Once the floor plan of exhibitors is finalised, a copy should be given to venue management so it can check that the plan meets with any health and safety requirements, such as leaving emergency exits clear. When the plan is approved, the actual display areas should be marked out with masking tape and the number and name of the exhibitor clearly marked on each.

The convener

The *convener* or organiser of a conference may be the board of management of a company, a steering committee appointed by the board of the company, or the supervisors or team leaders from different departments of a company. If a steering committee has been appointed to arrange the conference, members should have a good working knowledge of the topics to be discussed, and understand the requirements of management with regard to specific outcomes and the style of conference which is to be organised.

To **convene** means to 'cause to assemble for a specific purpose'; 'to gather or summon for a meeting'.

Some very large organisations employ conference staff who have been trained by professional event managers specifically for this task. This would be the case in some companies that mount several large events each year as part of their total marketing strategy.

EXERCISE 1

1. Name two topics you are likely to hear discussed at a formal conference.

_____

_____

_____

_____

2. Where would you be likely to find the rules which govern a formal conference?

_____

_____

_____

3. Would an interested member of the public be able to gain entrance to a conference arranged exclusively for members of an association? Explain why or why not.

_____

_____

_____

_____

_____

_____

_____

4. What is another phrase for 'a group of people of the same occupation'?

_____

_____

_____

_____

_____

5. If a conference was held *biennially*, how frequently would this be?

_____

_____

6. List six positive outcomes a publisher could gain from attending and displaying their books at a teachers' conference.

_____

_____

_____

_____

_____

_____

7. If you were part of a steering committee selected to organise a conference for your company, what would you need to have, apart from good organising capabilities?

_____

_____

_____

_____

8. If you were responsible for organising an exhibition as part of your company's conference, describe all the details you would need to supply to an exhibitor after they had booked a display space.

_____

_____

_____

_____

_____

_____

_____

1.2 Conference facilities requirements, budget and preparation timeline are confirmed

The facilities requirements to be confirmed with the conveners will vary, as much will depend on the size of the conference, its purpose and style, its duration and location. However some or all of the following will need to be taken into consideration when planning the conference:

- the room size;
- amenities and décor;
- equipment;
- stationery;
- catering arrangements; and
- parking.

Room size

The conference may require a space the size of an auditorium, a ballroom or a boardroom to accommodate the number of attendees. Based on how many people are expected, a suitable space would need to be identified. In the case of a company conference, the number of attendees (give or take a few) will be known very early in the planning stages.

If it is planned to have a variety of different sessions running concurrently, then appropriate arrangements will need to be made. In this case, a venue such as a hotel or conference centre which provides such facilities as a large hall with smaller meeting rooms nearby should be identified. An advantage of booking a hotel for the conference is that overnight accommodation is often provided at a special 'conference rate' for delegates.

Alternatively, many universities offer a choice of conference facilities at a reasonable price. These can vary from basic lecture theatres to modern, purpose-built conference suites. One advantage of using university facilities is that during the holiday periods, student accommodation may be booked by delegates at an extremely low price. However, the standard of the accommodation can vary considerably between campuses.

Amenities and decor

The venue should be well-lit and air-conditioned, with appropriate comfortable seating for the expected number of attendees. When assessing the suitability of the room or rooms, ensure there will be adequate space for the different seating plans that may be requested by presenters. It will also be necessary to work out how many rooms will be required.

For example, the conference may need one large room arranged in theatre style for the *plenary* sessions, and, if the delegates will later split up into smaller groups for workshops or special interest group presentations, several smaller rooms will be needed as well. These smaller rooms are often referred to as 'syndicate rooms'.

Ideally, these rooms would be situated in close *proximity* to the main conference hall. If they are not, and it will be necessary for delegates to use the lifts or stairs, you should ask about the availability of wheelchair access. Also, make sure adequate signage will be provided in *strategic* positions so attendees can find the rooms easily.

Floor plans: Maps or floor plans of the venue—showing where the rooms and other facilities (such as toilets) are situated, as well as where morning and afternoon teas and lunch will be served—would make a welcome addition to the delegates' conference satchels.

Furniture: The arrangement of the furniture will be dictated by the purpose and style of the conference and the number of attendees. If it is formal, with less than 50 attendees, the provision of a large table or an arrangement of a number of tables in an oval or u-shape so that everyone is able to see each other is important. Effective group interaction depends on easy eye contact, so all delegates should be able to see the speakers with ease.

Lighting: Lighting is also important. For example, if lights are dimmed during a presentation, with just a spotlight on the speaker, will there be sufficient light for delegates to take notes? Is there a light on the *lectern* so speakers can read their notes? In some venues, a control

Plenary means 'full or entire'; 'attended by all members'.

Proximity means 'nearness in place or time'.

Strategic means 'important or crucial to one's position'.

A *lectern* is a reading stand which holds a speaker's papers, prompt cards or notes, and often has a light attached to illuminate them.

panel is built into the speaker's lectern so they can control the lighting appropriately.

Power outlets: Adequate power outlets for equipment such as video projectors should be available in all rooms. If teleconferencing or videoconferencing equipment will be used, then phone lines will also be required.

If a trade display is being run as part of the conference, ensure that adequate space is available for the stands and sufficient power points are provided, as well as space for delegates to walk around comfortably and to establish any health and safety regulations which may be in force and followed by the venue management.

Equipment

All of the following may be required at a large conference. Certainly some of these items would be required at a conference of any size or style:

- audio-visual equipment;
- computer equipment;
- electronic whiteboards;
- microphones;
- teleconferencing speakers;
- flip charts;
- overhead projectors and screens;
- tape recorders;
- videoconferencing monitors and video cams;
- lecterns; and
- large overhead screen or monitors (if meeting is held in an auditorium).

It may be possible to hire some of this gear, so when venues are being considered as to their suitability find out what equipment is available—and whether there is an extra charge for its use.

Whether microphones will be necessary depends very much on the size of the auditorium and the acoustics. There may already be a sound system in place at the venue, but it is wise to check.

Stationery

A special letterhead may be designed, especially if the conference is a large and important event. Other stationery requirements at this stage may be the preparation and printing of registration forms and, later, copies of speeches and the programs or agendas for the conference.

Consideration could also be given as to whether writing pads and pens will be provided in delegates' conference satchels or at each place at the conference table, and whether these should have the conference name printed on them. Costs could be explored at this stage and printing quotes requested.

Catering arrangements

These will depend on the level of catering required. Naturally, the duration of the conference and the number of attendees would have a direct bearing on the level of catering, and thus, the costs.

Lunch and tea breaks: At a one-day conference, morning and afternoon teas and lunch would usually be provided to attendees. At longer conferences, delegates would be able to choose from food available at the venue or use nearby cafes or restaurants for meals. It is usual at all conferences to provide complimentary tea and coffee at the morning and afternoon breaks.

Dinner: Some conferences have an official dinner. The cost may be included in the fees; alternatively delegates must book and pay for attending the dinner.

Menus: A selection of sample menus and costs should be requested from the venue management for consideration by the conference committee. Make sure that the venue or the caterers you choose are able to provide meals for those on special diets, for example, vegetarians or diabetics. Also, decisions should be made as to whether the lunch will be eaten standing up or seated at tables. (Sitting down is usually more expensive.)

Parking

Limited parking may be available at the conference venue, or at nearby public car parks. If this is so, attendees should be provided with maps showing the exact location of entrances to the car parks. It would be well to find out whether the venue gives a discount on parking fees to conference delegates.

Australian Business Number

If the conference organiser is an association rather than a registered business or company, it may be necessary to register the organisation with the Australian Taxation Office and obtain an Australian Business Number.

Since the Federal Government introduced a Goods and Services Tax (GST) in 2000, all companies that collect money for a service or in exchange for goods must add a 10 per cent GST to the invoiced amount and subsequently *remit* this amount to the ATO together with the necessary paperwork.

Unless the organisation is *exempt* or has applied for an exemption from the ATO, it must have an Australian Business Number which should appear on all letterhead, invoices and receipts.

Budget planning

The costs or budget allocated for the conference should be established and confirmed before any arrangements are made. Normally, the company's financial director or accountant will allocate a certain amount, or set a limit on the amount of money to be spent on the conference, with the planning and decisions as to how the money is spent at the *discretion* of the organising committee. It may be possible to refer to the budgets of previous conferences for an indication of the likely costs involved.

If the conference is to be large or complex and therefore expensive, it would be advisable to use computer planning tools to manage the various components or cost centres. Software packages are available which provide budget control charts so that specific items can be identified and isolated to track and *monitor* their costs more easily. Many of these programs can be networked so others involved with the planning or organising can access and use the system.

*To **remit** means to 'transmit or send to a person or place'.*

*To be **exempt** means 'to be free from an obligation or liability to which others are subject'.*

*In this context, **discretion** means 'power or right of deciding'; 'acting according to one's own judgment'.*

*To **monitor** means 'to check, observe or record without interfering'.*

Draft budget—costs or outgoings

A draft budget should be prepared based on the convener's plan for the conference. The budget may be developed with the costs being calculated using estimates or preliminary quotes provided by suppliers and/or the expected cost of each task or requirement such as:

- venue hire;
- hire, delivery and set-up of equipment;
- catering;
- stationery and brochure design and printing;
- advertising and mailouts;
- travel and accommodation;
- information kits;
- printing of program and abstracts;
- speakers' fees (if any);
- gifts for speakers; and
- incidentals (name tags, satchels, pads, pens, flowers, signs etc).

Fixed and variable costs

Some of these costs will be **fixed**, no matter how many delegates will be at the conference. For instance:

- venue hire;
- stationery and brochure design;
- speakers' fees;
- travel and accommodation; and
- advertising/promotion.

Whereas some of the **variable costs** would be:

- catering;
- gifts for speakers; and
- name tags.

Draft budget—income

On the credit side, a decision should be made very early about setting a conference fee (where appropriate) and the amount that will be charged. Concessions may be offered to some participants, such as 'early bird' registrations and students, if that is applicable, and this should also be decided by the convener.

Fees will also be charged for the conference dinner and any excursions or other social activities arranged for delegates. (The fees usually cover the costs involved plus a small profit.)

Based on the expected number of attendees or delegates, an estimate can then be made as to whether the conference is likely to make a profit or *deficit* or break even. Hopefully it will deliver a modest surplus.

However, the final amount of profit or loss may change if, as described in *Combination of outcomes and purposes* on page 4, conference sponsors were *recruited* to help defray the costs of mounting the conference by, for example, providing items such as stationery, or paying fees to display their products at the conference or advertise in the conference program.

As with the costs, the income will be derived from various sources and therefore specific items can be identified as being **fixed** or **variable**.

Fixed income would come from, for example, the hire of display areas for a trade fair, sponsorship and advertising. An example of **variable** income would be the different fees paid by delegates.

Deficit means 'the amount by which a sum of money falls short of the required amount'.

To *recruit* means 'to newly secure a member or supporter of any body or class'.

Planning approaches to sponsors
It will be necessary to work out a plan to attract sponsors for the conference. For instance, if there is to be a trade fair or display in tandem with the conference, suitable companies should be approached early in the planning stages, offering them the opportunity to mount product displays, with different levels of costs depending on the size of the display space allocated to them.

Different types of sponsorship
The offer of different types of sponsorship could also be outlined, with a scale of suggested fees for each item. Sponsors can then

choose the amount of money they think is appropriate to spend on promoting their company or products at that particular conference. Some may prefer just to be one of the sponsors of the conference, others may choose only to display their products at the trade show. And some may choose to do both.

Sponsors do not have to be confined to companies directly associated or affiliated with the theme of the conference. Large corporations whose businesses have no relationship to the organisation arranging the conference often sponsor a conference, so virtually any large company may be approached for support as well. Their requirements would be similar to other companies—prominence of their company name and logo in exchange for their financial support.

There are many such opportunities, so long as the sponsor is satisfied it is getting value for money. That is why it is important to be very clear when approaching sponsors as to what benefits will be given for different levels of sponsorship. Normally, the organisers would produce a list of events or items that were available for sponsorship along with the cost so that the companies may select those appropriate to their interests or budget. For example:

- Providing wines for the conference dinner.
- Printing the menus.
- Providing flowers and table decorations.
- Providing notepads for delegates' satchels.
- Printing the abstracts and conference program.

(The estimated number of menus or brochures required can be provided to the sponsor early on and then confirmed closer to the date, when registrations have been received and the number of attendees is known.)

The names and logos of all major sponsors would be displayed on all conference mailing brochures and in the program, including the airlines and the hotels that have agreed to provide discounted services for the conference. Minor sponsors' names would be displayed as the conference committee decides but would be listed in the program. Here are some examples:

- The menus would bear the logo and name of the printing sponsor.
- Small cards or signs would be placed on the dinner tables identifying the companies providing the wines and table decorations.

If this has been arranged, then sponsors' logos and artwork for advertisements should be requested well in advance so as not to delay publication of the program.

Of course, the amount of prominence required by sponsors should always be open to negotiation and the foregoing are only simple examples. It is usual practice to offer each sponsor two free conference places, which would allow them entry to any of the sessions. It is also usual practice that the names of all sponsors and those companies mounting a display at the trade show be listed at the back of the conference program.

How much to charge sponsors

The usual way of calculating the charge is based on the actual cost of each item with a percentage added which is deemed to be the sponsor's contribution. (The amount will vary according to the type of conference and the circumstances.)

Presenting a workshop

Some sponsors of the conference may be permitted to present a session, at the discretion of the organising committee, but sponsors should be encouraged to make these more than just selling sessions. An example would be at an English teachers' conference where the publisher of a new series of textbooks or reading program would provide a session so the author(s) could workshop the new system and discuss the research methods used and the benefits for teachers and pupils in its use.

Confirming sponsorship arrangements

Once an agreement has been reached with a sponsor, a letter of confirmation should be sent outlining the level of sponsorship, the agreed fee, and exactly what benefits the sponsor will be given (e.g. the prominence of the company name and logo). It would also confirm whether artwork for brochures etc. which includes the company's logo will need to be submitted to them for approval before printing.

The sponsor should be invoiced before an item is ordered (e.g. conference satchels with the sponsor's name overprinted on them) and when they are delivered, a sample should be sent to the sponsor with a compliments slip or note.

Conference preparation timeline

The amount of lead time required for preparations and arrangements to be made will depend very much on the size and scale of the conference. Some conferences may require a lead time of nine months or more, while others may require only a few weeks.

Drawing up a timeline which shows when each task is to be completed is an effective way for the organising committee to see what is required to be done, when each task is to be completed, and by whom. The timeline could be displayed as a large wall chart, or prepared and updated regularly on a computer network. There are many ways of creating this sort of timeline, but here is a simple example.

First, following the confirmation of the date for the conference, its purpose, theme and style, it would be necessary to list all of the tasks or details to be dealt with in a rough order of priority, such as:

1. Organise keynote speakers and presenters.
2. Obtain biographies and photographs of all speakers.
3. Draft the program.
4. Call for abstracts of papers.
5. Organise excursion details.
6. Decide on fees for exhibition stands.
7. Prepare brochures and mailings.
8. Build and put up a web site and update regularly.
9. Approach potential sponsors.
10. Book the venue.
11. List equipment needs.
12. Organise catering.
13. Organise accommodation for speakers.
14. Record expressions of interest.
15. Allocate rooms for sessions.
16. Appoint chairs or mediators for sessions.
17. Confirm and finalise the program details.
18. Print program.
19. Pack delegates' satchels.
20. Prepare registration desks.

Note: This is not an exhaustive list, nor are the items in strict order of priority as every conference will have different requirements, expected outcomes and styles.

The tasks would then be arranged in groups under time categories headings. These headings would indicate the amount of time before the conference date that the tasks in the list must be dealt with or finalised, such as: **9 months 6 months 3 months 3 weeks 10 days 1 week 5 days 3 days.**

So, under the **6 months** heading you may find:

- ❑ Prepare list of speakers to be approached.

- ❑ Letterhead to be printed.

- ❑ List excursion destinations to be considered.

- ❑ Design web site.

- ❑ Approach possible sponsors.

Following discussions, the various tasks will be shared out so that, beside each item on the list, the name of the individual or group whose responsibility it is to complete the task will be noted along with the completion date.

Fortunately, not all conferences require so much advance planning or intricate organisation. However, whatever the scope and size of a conference, even a one-day event, the organiser(s) must be meticulous and make sure they have a plan of organisation so that arrangements, and the conference itself, run smoothly.

Outside help

Some companies find it helpful to employ a freelance professional conference organiser to assist with or take over the management of certain aspects of the arrangements. This can be cost-efficient and prove very beneficial in freeing up some of their employees who might otherwise spend much time organising the company's conference when they could be working at their usual jobs.

EXERCISE 2

1. List five factors which would influence the type of facilities that would be required in a conference venue.

_____

_____

_____

_____

_____

2. If several workshops at a conference were held *concurrently*, what would this mean?

_____

_____

_____

3. Explain what 'effective group interaction' means.

_____

_____

_____

_____

4. Before any firm arrangements or bookings are made for a conference, what is the first thing that should be established and confirmed?

_____

_____

_____

_____

5. How would this be done?

_____

_____

6. Describe how you would begin to prepare and then calculate the draft budget or costs for a conference.

_____

_____

_____

_____

_____

7. What is the meaning of the term 'early bird fee'?

_____

_____

8. How would a calculation be made as to whether a conference is likely to make a profit or deficit?

_____

_____

_____

_____

9. In your own words, describe a 'preparation timeline' and how you would use one.

_____

_____

_____

_____

_____

_____

_____

10. Apart from promoting a company's name and profile to delegates, what other benefits could a sponsor receive at a conference?

_____

_____

_____

_____

1.3 Speakers are identified and a call for papers is prepared

Identifying and then securing the services of the right speaker or speakers is very important. Speakers can make or break a conference. The *keynote* speaker sets the tone of the event, and should be stimulating—even entertaining—and therefore must be chosen with care.

In this context, a **keynote** is 'that which relates to or defines the main interest or determining principle of a conference'.

Motivational comes from the word 'motivate' which means 'something that prompts a person to act in a certain way'; 'the goal or purpose of one's actions'.

A list of possible speakers should be prepared as early as possible, because some popular and thus sought-after keynote or *motivational* speakers or those with a high profile in their field of expertise are often booked up a year in advance, and may not be available on the date when the organisation requires them.

Therefore, the list of potential presenters and speakers should not be limited to a few 'top' names to allow for those who may be unavailable. And the chosen one (or two) should be approached as soon as possible. Successful conference organisers choose and book their speakers six to 12 months in advance to have a wide range of choice.

Where to find them

The National Speakers Association of Australia (NSAA) has a web site containing a directory of speakers—*Who's Who in Professional Speaking in Australia*—which could be an effective way to find suitable presenters. The site also lists recommended speakers' bureaus or agencies to help you work through lists of speakers of whom you may never have heard. There is no charge for finding a speaker in this way because the bureaus charge their speakers a commission on fees received.

Speakers' fees

If you plan to engage a professional keynote speaker, the fee you may be expected to pay can range between $3,000 and $6,000 for an hour's presentation. Any travel and accommodation would be extra.

In-house speakers

On the other hand, if the speakers are to be drawn from the company's own staff members and associates such as team leaders, divisional heads or directors, then a much shorter lead time would be appropriate for ensuring their availability. A list of possible speakers would be drawn up in the same way for consideration by the organisers and management. In general, all speakers should be articulate, knowledgeable about their subject, well prepared and able to hold the audience's attention.

The theme and title of the conference

At this point, or when the initial discussions are taking place about the conference, a theme and a title for the conference should be agreed on. This would obviously relate to the purpose and nature of the conference.

For example, 'Extending the Boundaries: The Heightened Role of Career Planning in Knowledge Societies' or 'The Way Forward: Marketing Strategies for the New Millennium' or '4th International Conference on Drugs and Young People: Focusing on Solutions'.

Once the theme and title have been decided, the conference logo and letterhead can be designed and prepared for approval. The logo and theme/title should appear on all printed matter for the conference such as fliers, posters, the program, printed *abstracts* as well as the web site.

*An **abstract** is a 'summary of a statement of speech'.*

Call for papers

In the case of an association, an invitation to attend the conference, or at this early stage to register interest in doing so, and a call for papers should be sent to all members. (The purpose of asking members to register interest in attending is to help the organisers gauge the possible number of attendees, as many of the arrangements will depend on this number.)

The invitation could be in the form of a letter or a leaflet and may be emailed or sent as a special mailing to members through the normal postal system. It would be important to convey as much information as possible, including the date and location as well as the purpose, style and theme of the conference, even if it is apparent from the title. For example,

The **Purpose:** presenting and sharing research findings about the impact of alcohol and other drugs on the lives of young people.

The **Style:** formal and of four days' duration.

The **Theme:** focusing on solutions to the problems.

The **Date:** December 1–4, 2004.

The **Location:** Perth Convention Centre.

A notice or advertisement could also be placed in suitable journals, sent to university departments and posted on a web site to attract possible presenters.

The call for papers may provide details about the various streams of the conference (where applicable), so that speakers can choose one that best fits their area of interest or expertise. For example: 'Alcohol and other drug use patterns and cultures'; 'Prevention and health promotion'; 'Early intervention'; 'Research'; 'Legal issues'.

Some conferences would require potential presenters to complete an official abstract form that also contained instructions for them about their submissions. Thus information may be provided about how the abstract is to be submitted—how many words and what it should contain; the format—hard copy or electronic; and the closing date for submissions. The speaker may be required to indicate the preferred length and the format of their presentation (e.g. paper/oral, debate, skills transfer), as well as any specific audio-visual or other equipment they may require.

A brief career biography would usually be expected to accompany the abstract, and a photograph of the presenter for possible use in the program or advertisements for the conference.

Selection

All submissions would then be assessed by independent reviewers or members of the program committee as to their relevance and interest to delegates, and those most worthy or interesting would be chosen.

All presenters should be advised of the decisions made about their abstracts within a certain period set down by the conference committee.

Keynote speakers: If keynote speakers are to be invited, they should be given a longer time to prepare than those submitting and presenting papers, and encouraged to present new thoughts and ideas in their talk. They should be sent a request for their biography and photo, an abstract of their address and a copyright release form.

Some members of parliament or government ministers will often speak at conferences, usually delivering the keynote address at the first plenary session. This can attract media coverage for the conference, if that is desirable. As MPs and ministers' diaries are often quite full, it is wise to approach them well in advance of the date of the conference.

Copyright release form

All speakers should be asked to sign a copyright release form. This document simply grants permission to the conference organisers to publish the full text of a speaker's paper in the publication of the proceedings, which is produced after a conference has finished. This can either be a bound hard copy and/or a CD-ROM.

The permission would be limited to 'first publication rights only'—that is, the author of the paper would be free to publish it elsewhere in the future. In signing the release form, the author grants a once-only use of their work to the conference committee.

EXERCISE 3

1. Why would the selection of a keynote speaker be so important?

_____

_____

_____

_____

2. Why would you ask possible delegates to a conference to register an interest in attending nine months ahead of the date of the event?

_____

_____

_____

3. How would you do this? Give two methods.

_____

_____

4. What information should this communication to possible delegates and speakers contain?

_____

_____

_____

_____

5. What is an 'abstract'?

_____

_____

6. Apart from an abstract, what else should you request potential speakers to send you?

_____

_____

_____

_____

7. Why do you think keynote speakers would be given a longer period to prepare their presentations?

_____

_____

_____

_____

_____

_____

_____

_____

8. What is the purpose of a copyright release form as it would apply to papers presented at a conference?

_____

_____

_____

_____

9. Select a partner to work with. You have been given the task of creating a theme and a snappy but informative title for your company's upcoming conference. The conference is on the subject of **Cars of the Future**; its purpose is to focus on green alternatives to the use of fossil fuels. The attendees are expected to be possible manufacturers, retailers and representatives from government. The style will be semi-formal. Speakers will be experts in the field, and some workshops will be hands-on with demonstrations of some prototypes.

Take 10 minutes to brainstorm with your partner and come up with some ideas. List them, if you have more than one theme and title, and then prepare a list of the main streams or topics that could be covered at the conference. Compare with other groups.

_____

_____

_____

_____

_____

_____

_____

_____

_____

_____

1.4 Conference program is drafted in line with stated purpose; choice of program elements is balanced to allow outcomes to be achieved

1.5 Speakers are selected, invited and briefed in accordance with the conference program
(These two units have been combined because they are interdependent.)

Once the purpose and style of the conference have been clarified, a program for the conference will be drafted, bearing in mind the required outcomes. The draft should be appropriate to the stated purpose of the conference, and the various elements of the program balanced so that an interesting range of sessions is offered. The arrangement of the program should also allow adequate time for each main topic.

Program elements
The program elements may include some or all of the following:

- Plenary sessions
- Presentations
- Lectures
- Workshops
- Small group discussions
- Question-and-answer sessions with a panel
- Video or PowerPoint presentations
- Demonstrations
- Practice sessions
- Team-building exercises

Some conference venues provide team-building activities such as abseiling, a high rope course, an obstacle course, hang-gliding and bushwalking. Depending on the occasion, the committee may decide to integrate some of these activities into the overall program.

Social program
At some conferences, an outing with some professional *relevance* or input or an excursion to a local site of interest is often arranged, usually in the middle of the conference, to break up the sessions of papers.

Other aspects of the social program for delegates and their partners may consist of the conference dinner, a pre-conference activity such as a welcoming cocktail party, and perhaps one or two other functions, depending on the duration of the conference and the number of attendees. Some functions are inclusive of the conference fee while others require further payment, usually settled at the time of registration.

The social program has its value apart from the merely *recreational*, as it offers delegates the opportunity to network with colleagues in a relaxed and informal setting.

Accompanying persons program

A program for partners or accompanying persons is often provided at large conferences, particularly if the conference is being held at a location of historical interest or great beauty. A fee is charged for this and events such as sightseeing tours. The tours are best provided by local professional guides rather than by volunteers, as value for money is important.

Conference sponsors

If it has been agreed to invite sponsors to support the conference, approaches should be made at this stage of the preparations. The organisers should be very clear when approaching sponsors as to what benefits will attach to different levels of sponsorship as described on page 15 under *Planning approaches to sponsors*. A full description of the process can be found in this section of the book.

Selection and briefing of speakers

After the deadline for submission of abstracts of papers has closed, the selection process begins. The program committee or the person responsible for managing this part of the conference will review all the submitted abstracts and decide which appear to be the most suitable for the purpose and required outcomes, so that the final program can be designed.

In or out

Authors of papers should be informed as soon as possible after the decision has been made as to whether they are to be included in the conference or not. It would be appropriate to request that authors who have been selected submit a copy of their complete paper or

Relevance means 'bearing upon or connected with the matter in hand'.

Recreational means 'refreshing by means of some pastime or the like'; 'diversionary or affording relaxation and enjoyment'..

presentation one month before the conference, together with the completed copyright release form. The letter should also provide details about the conference and some background information about the organisation and its aims and objectives, if the speaker is not a member.

The same would apply in the case of a business, with perhaps some brief history of the company and a summary of the type of people who will make up the audience, to allow the speaker to prepare their presentation to suit the delegates.

In the letter, include a request for speakers to inform you of any special dietary requirements they may have—e.g. allergies to certain foods—and include a map showing the location of the venue and parking station[s], and give directions as to where they are to go on arrival.

It would be appropriate at this point to check that the biographical details and photograph of each presenter have been received for inclusion in the program and, if not, they should be reminded of the deadline for submission.

Financial and other arrangements for speakers

If appropriate, the details of the financial arrangements should be confirmed at this time—that is, if they are charging a fee—as well as any travel or accommodation bookings that need to be made for them.

Make clear what is being provided—for example, "We confirm that we shall pay you a speaker honorarium of $300 as well as providing bed and breakfast at the Gateway Hotel and airline tickets to and from Melbourne. Please note that you will be responsible for all other expenses."

Speakers should be asked if they will require any particular equipment for their presentations such as a whiteboard, flip chart or video equipment and, if so, these requirements should be noted and filed for later reference when the syndicate rooms are being allocated for sessions.

When the program has been finalised, formatted and is ready to go to press, each presenter should be advised of the time and date they will be speaking (if the conference is spread over several days), and the name of the chair or moderator of their session.

1.6 Participant target group and projected numbers are identified

If the conference is an 'in-house' function—that is, one involving only employees of the company and perhaps invited speakers—then the identities and the number of attendees will be known. Similarly, if the conference is a formal affair, either large or small, with invited delegates from various branches of a company or organisation, then the identities and number attending will be easy to calculate with almost total accuracy.

Numbers unknown but projected

If the conference is that of an association or large organisation and is held annually or biennially, then the organisers will have an *idea* of the approximate number of people likely to attend, based on previous attendance numbers. Once expressions of interest to attend and registrations begin to come in, the organisers may be able to 'guesstimate' the numbers.

It is always difficult to calculate accurately the number of people who will attend conferences such as this, but it is necessary to be as accurate as possible because of arrangements such as catering and seating which must be confirmed.

Incentives for early registration

One way of encouraging people to register early for a conference is to offer discounts for 'early bird' registrations, as well as providing credit card facilities. The early bird registration offer would usually close two or even three months before the date of the conference, thus giving the organisers some of the vital information they need. Ordinary registrations would close 14 days before the conference, although late registration would usually be accepted.

Another factor which may tip the balance of attendance over non-attendance is whether deals can be arranged for reduced rates on accommodation and air fares for delegates. This is frequently done, and the details and options are usually presented on mailouts and registration forms. (See example under the **Registration procedures** heading in section 1.7: *Administration requirements are analysed* ... on page 36.)

A way of gauging early interest levels would be to keep track of the number of hits to the conference web site (if one is set up and monitored). Designing a registration form that can be downloaded from the web site is another way of making registration more straightforward. Obviously, this would only apply to a large conference where not just members or employees are able to register and attend.

The number of attendees at a large conference would increase if sponsors were involved in a trade display as part of the conference because representatives of the companies participating may plan to attend some or all of the sessions. These possible attendees would need to be taken into account when calculating the numbers for seating and catering arrangements.

EXERCISE 4

1. If you were drafting a program for a conference, list the three qualities that it should contain.

_____

_____

_____

_____

_____

_____

_____

2. List five team-building activities you could participate in at some conference venues.

_____

_____

_____

_____

_____

_____

_____

3. Give two reasons why an outing or excursion might be arranged in the middle of a conference.

_____

_____

_____

_____

_____

_____

_____

_____

4. What would be a possible benefit of an excursion to delegates?

_____

_____

_____

_____

5. Why would you hire professional guides to escort visitors on an excursion? Give two reasons.

_____

_____

_____

_____

6. Why do you think the conference organisers should be very clear about the different levels of benefits extended to sponsors?

_____

_____

_____

_____

7. If you were a speaker selected to give a presentation at a conference, what sort of information or directions could you reasonably expect to receive from the conference organisers? Name seven.

_____

_____

_____

_____

_____

_____

_____

8. If you were responsible for arranging the speakers for a conference, what sort of information and documents would you require from them? Name five.

_____

_____

_____

_____

_____

9. What do you think 'guesstimate' means?

_____

_____

10. What are two ways of encouraging delegates to register for a conference as soon as they find out about it?

_____

_____

_____

_____

11. If you found out about a conference you really wanted to attend, but it was two days before it was to commence, could you still register and attend?

_____

12. What are two ways of gauging the possible number of attendees at a conference?

_____

_____

_____

_____

_____

_____

_____

_____

_____

1.7 Administration requirements are analysed and tasks, processes and resources planned

To ensure efficient management of the conference data and resources, administration requirements may include some or all of the following:

- a conference web page;
- registration procedures;
- cash management and budgetary control; and
- preparation of evaluation questionnaires.

Conference web page

If a web page is to be designed and mounted (often done for big conferences), this should be arranged as early as possible after the conference date has been set, but usually not more than 12 months in advance. The page should include an invitation to attend and, in the case of an association, a call for abstracts of papers to be submitted for consideration as described earlier.

To aid those who may be interested, the following could be included on the page: '..further details will be posted on this site towards the end of..' with the inclusion of the projected date of the next update—regular updates are very important. In the next update, the title and theme of the conference should be added, if they were not given earlier, along with known details about some or all of the following:

Preliminary means 'leading up to'; 'occurring before or in preparation for an activity'.

- an outline of the *preliminary* program or confirmed program highlights;
- planned or confirmed social program;
- titles of speakers' papers and the speakers' biographical information; and
- a request for expressions of interest to attend.

(This would usually be a request from interested parties to be placed on a mailing list to be sent further information and a registration form, as they become available.)

Registration procedures

About six months out from the date of the conference, an online registration form and/or one which can be downloaded should be added to the web site. This would include a list of the scale of fees and a special discount offer for early bird registrations and, if possible, offering credit card facilities.

For example: "If you want to register for the conference using any of these cards [list credit cards], simply indicate the kind of card you wish to use and write your name and card number, along with the expiry date, on our printable registration form and then sign as indicated."

The scale of fees would naturally vary from conference to conference, in fact some conferences, such as those which are an annual company conference, would not make any charges at all. However, if fees are to be charged the registration form will contain various items to be completed, such as some or all of the following shown on the sample form on the next page.

Some registration forms spell out exactly what is included in the cost, as in the example. And it is always advisable to show the final date for cancellation refunds on the form.

Cash management and budgetary control

It is important that all the arrangements for any conference, whether partially funded by delegates' fees or not, are placed within cost centres and that each item does not exceed its individual allocated budget, if this is the way the company plans to handle the financial aspects. However, all ongoing costs and expenses should be carefully monitored and recorded.

As discussed earlier, under the heading *Combination of outcomes and purposes* on page 4, where suitable, some organisers, particularly of those conferences arranged by professional associations rather than commercial enterprises, will invite commercial organisations allied to the purpose and style of the conference to mount displays of their products for an agreed fee to help fund the conference. Also, as already described, sponsorship for the conference or particular aspects of the conference may be sought to assist with the costs.

REGISTRATION FORM

Complete this form and post with a cheque, postmarked by May 1, 2003 to receive the 'Early Bird' fee. A copy of this form may also be e-mailed (address) or faxed (fax number) with credit card details. Please print or type and post to: (address)

Name_____

Company or Institution_____

Address_____

Phone_____ Fax_____ E-mail_____

Special dietary requirements_____

Registration Fees include morning and afternoon teas, entry to all sessions, awards lunch, conference materials.

Early Bird $455____ Regular $530____ Daily Rate $160____

Optional extras: Conference dinner $70____ Excursion $50____

Name on credit card_____

Signature_____

Expiry date_____ Total payment $_____

Cancellation Policy Cancellations must be requested in writing and post-marked no later than June 4, 2003.

Travel Information For special discounted conference travel arrangements on Qantas, phone [number] and use the Silver File Account when booking.

Hotel Reservations These hotels are offering discounted rates for the conference (to obtain these rates you must book through Jetset Travel): Holiday Inn [address] $100 a night; Hampton Towers [address] $80 a night.

For GST purposes this registration form will become a TAX INVOICE when paid in full. Visit our web site for conference updates—www.ozbkpub.com.au

REGISTRATIONS CLOSE JUNE 4

Tasks, processes and resources planning

The many tasks to be completed and the methods used to *accomplish* them will be decided, administered and monitored by the organising committee of the conference. If necessary, other employees or individuals may be *co-opted* onto the committee for a certain period to assist in a particular area which requires their special knowledge or expertise.

All tasks should be allocated early in the planning stage so those concerned are aware of their responsibilities and the timeframe in which they must accomplish them. Regular meetings, where updates and progress reports are given, should be arranged to ensure everything is on track.

Most important of all, meticulous records must be kept of such things as:

- all decisions made;
- tasks allocated and to whom;
- deadlines for accomplishment of tasks;
- quotes received for services such as catering and equipment hire;
- sponsors approached; and
- financial arrangements made with speakers.

Information/registration desk

In the case of a large conference, a *roster* would need to be drawn up for the first day, listing the times and names of those responsible for manning the registration desks to welcome delegates and to hand out satchels containing the program or agenda, receipts for fees paid, individual name tags, a map of the venue and other information *relevant* to the conference.

On following days, other personnel would be rostered to sit at the conference information desk to provide assistance and answer questions.

It is often desirable to have the registration desks open on the afternoon before the start of the conference for early arrivals, and particularly if there is to be a pre-conference activity such as welcoming drinks in the evening. The information desk should have local tourism information and maps available for delegates not familiar with the area.

To **accomplish** means 'to manage to do, to achieve'.

To **co-opt** means 'to add to a group with the agreement of the existing members'.

A **roster** is 'a list showing the order in which people are to perform a duty'.

Relevant means 'bearing upon or to do with the matter in hand'.

Fewer helpers would be needed on the day before and on the day or days following the first day of the conference.

Preparation of evaluation questionnaire

At some conferences, an evaluation questionnaire is distributed to all attendees for completion and return to the information desk and/or handed in to organisers after the last session. The comments are usually *anonymous*, because no names or addresses are required. In this way, the organisers can be sure they will receive *candid* responses to the questions.

Anonymous means 'by someone whose name is unknown'.

The purpose of the questionnaire is to gain genuine feedback from delegates about specific or sometimes all aspects of the conference so that the next one can be improved or changed, if necessary. The form may contain questions about the standard of the presentations, suitability of the venue and so on. Here are some further ideas that could be included in the questionnaire.

Candid means 'honest and straightforward'.

However, to be effective and meet the needs of the conference organisers, a questionnaire does not need to be as searching in its examination of delegates as the following list may suggest:

- Pre-conference information—how delegates found out about the conference, and if it contained sufficient detail.
- Fee structure—too high? Reasonable?
- Ease of registration—for conference, on arrival.
- The way the conference was organised: Satisfactory? Good? Poor?
- The standard of presenters and/or sessions.
- The relevance and duration of sessions.
- Whether the topic or theme of the conference was dealt with in a satisfactory way.
- Whether the content was stimulating and informative.
- Was the trade display interesting and appropriate (if one was mounted).

Any comments about the way the conference was handled by the organisers. This could be broken down into specifics such as:

- Punctuality.
- Ease of finding sessions rooms.
- Availability of information.
- Any comments about the program?
- Are there any particular topics you would like to be addressed at future conferences?
- Any other comments?

Designing the evaluation form

There are many methods of writing and designing a questionnaire. Some people consider it is best left to experts trained in this field, such as market researchers or psychologists, to gain unbiased and helpful information from those surveyed. However, if the conference is not large, particularly one arranged for the staff of an organisation, then having the questionnaire written and printed in-house could produce satisfactory results.

The use of a simple marking system such as circling one of several options or ticking boxes to answer many questions makes the task quicker and the form easier for delegates to complete. A rating system between 1 and 5 could be included to evaluate individual speakers' presentations.

Remind delegates to complete the evaluation form

At intervals during the conference, the chairperson should remind delegates not to overlook completing and handing in the form so the organisers can use the feedback to improve next year's conference.

EXERCISE 5

1. If you had registered your interest in attending a conference to be held in nine months' time, what would you expect to happen?

_____

_____

_____

_____

_____

_____

_____

2. What sort of conferences are unlikely to charge a fee for attendance?

_____

_____

3. If you were attending a four-day conference in another State, what sort of discounted expenses could you pay for when you registered for the conference?

_____

_____

_____

_____

_____

_____

4. Could you pay for these over the Internet with your credit card?

_____

5. Why would it be important to update the conference web site at regular intervals?

_____

_____

_____

_____

_____

6. Describe how you would monitor conferences expenses.

_____

_____

_____

_____

_____

_____

7. List three ways that the organising committee could ensure that the conference administration runs smoothly.

_____

_____

_____

8. What functions would the people at the registration desks perform? List five.

_____

_____

_____

_____

_____

_____

_____

9. Why would the organisers hand out evaluation questionnaires to delegates at a conference?

_____

_____

_____

_____

_____

_____

_____

_____

_____

_____

10. What types of people may be employed to design and write an evaluation questionnaire? Give two professions.

_____

_____

_____

_____

2 Promote the conference

In this element, different types of promotional strategies for conferences are considered. Various aspects are discussed, including print advertising, 'advertorial', press releases and press coverage and mailings to potential delegates. Different methods of mailing are also considered.

Next, details about the actual production of brochures or leaflets are examined and the types of options that may be available.

Alternative promotional methods such as the Internet and professional publicists are also touched on.

2.1 A promotion strategy is established that reaches required number of target participants

2.2 Publicity material is prepared and dispatched within designated timelines

(These two units have been combined because they are interdependent.)

The promotion strategy will need to take into account some or all of the following:

- The purpose and nature of the conference.
- Targeting relevant industry groups.
- Number of participants attending.
- Date, time and location of the conference.
- Providing adequate notice and coverage.

Beginning early

If, for example, the conference is an ongoing annual event and not an in-house or 'for staff only' type of gathering, the date and time of the following year's conference should be announced at the closing session of the preceding conference. The date, time and venue and any other details such as the nature or purpose of the conference could also be printed at the end of the program as a reminder.

Where it is appropriate, a brief presentation, perhaps prepared in PowerPoint or a similar computer application, could be shown and/or flyers printed and handed out at the closing session of the preceding conference to advertise the next one, even if its theme and purpose have not yet been confirmed.

Print advertising

Members of a particular profession or trade could be reached through taking out advertisements in trade journals, magazines and newsletters to announce the conference some months before its date. The ads could be inserted regularly, with the amount of information increasing or changing as arrangements and speakers are confirmed.

Closer to the date of the conference, and in line with the organising committee's plans, a registration form could be added to the advertisement or printed separately and inserted in the magazine. Naturally, the budget allocated for promotion would have a bearing on how many advertisements could be placed in this way.

Daily newspapers

If the conference has been fortunate enough to secure a very well known and highly respected keynote speaker such as, for example, Canada's Dr David Suzuki, a display advertisement of modest proportions, say, 7cm x 8cm could be designed to promote the speaker as much as the conference. It could look like this:

```
┌──────────────────────────────────────┐
│  ┌────────────────────────────────┐  │
│  │   FUTURE OF THE PLANET         │  │
│  │   CONFERENCE                   │  │
│  └────────────────────────────────┘  │
│         KEYNOTE SPEAKER               │
│                                        │
│        DR DAVID SUZUKI                 │
│                                        │
│       Thursday, June 23, 2003          │
│   Oceania Centre, No 1 Xana Place, Sydney │
│         $330 (including GST)           │
│        For bookings please call        │
│         AUSTRALIAN FORUM OF            │
│       DEVELOPMENTAL RESEARCH           │
│           (02) 9091 1234               │
│                                        │
│  ┌────────────────────────────────┐  │
│  │ Sponsorship details: (02) 9991 4567 │  │
│  └────────────────────────────────┘  │
└──────────────────────────────────────┘
```

Advertorial

Some magazines may agree to give a certain amount free space to the conference if an article, usually referred to as 'copy', is supplied to them for publication. This would need to be typed neatly, in double spacing, with generous margins on either side of each page. However, some magazines require an advertisement to be bought in return for extra space elsewhere in the magazine in the form of an article. This is usually referred to as 'advertorial'.

Whatever the financial arrangement agreed on, a short article could be written explaining the purpose of the conference and listing the names of the confirmed speakers, along with any interesting biographical details of some of them. In addition, any highlights or arrangements that could attract readers to register for the conference should be included in the article. Naturally, the information contained in the article will not mirror exactly the text of the advertisements, apart from the date, venue and theme or title of the conference.

Alternatively, if one or more well-known or high-profile speakers were participating in the conference, then an article could be written about them, or if an interview were possible, then the text of the interview, if it is considered to be appropriate, could be submitted. Any such article would naturally include details about the date, theme and location of the conference.

Free promotion - press releases

Using local and interstate newspapers to run a story about the conference is another approach that could be tried. A well-written press release may be published in a daily or weekly paper, particularly if the topic is of general interest and not just of appeal to a narrow field of possible participants. If a well-known or highly qualified speaker is attending the conference this can be a hook on which to hang the story.

The press release could be sent to all media, not just print: radio, TV current affairs programs, news editors, breakfast shows, talk shows and so on. It should be clear, concise and appealing, with the specific details listed in point form at the beginning so the recipient does not have to search through masses of text to find the point. Include any photographs of interesting speakers and a copy of the conference brochure or draft program.

If a spokesperson from the organising committee or a director of the company could be available for interview, so much the better. This should be indicated at the top or bottom of the release along with contact names and phone numbers.

When sending a release it is important to address it to the person you want to read it. In many cases you would send it to a TV or radio interviewer's producer, not the 'talking head', or the news editor of a program or the news or features editor of a newspaper—but it always helps to have a *name*. Generally, it's a good idea to phone the person a few days after the release has been sent to follow up and see if they intend using the story or are interested in arranging an interview.

Mailings

Depending on the budget allocated for promotion, brochures announcing the conference, its purpose and nature, and containing details about speakers and other arrangements could be prepared and mailed to target participants. The brochures should include a registration form or a separate registration leaflet to be completed and returned by a due date.

As discussed earlier, offering a discount on the fee for early registration is an incentive for interested parties to make a decision earlier rather than later (see sample registration form on page 38.)

If the promotional budget allows it, several mailings could be done using differently designed brochures. The first leaflet would announce the basic details and preliminary program of the conference and the names of any speakers, if they are known. Then a month or so later, a further mailing containing more information and highlights of the conference could be sent out. Both mail-outs would include a registration form.

Another approach could be for the second mailing to contain a list of all the confirmed speakers and presenters and the topics of the papers they will present, together with the biographical notes they supplied. This approach would be better suited to a conference organised by a professional body or association such as a medical or book publishers' conference.

Producing the brochures/leaflets

A well-designed, attractive and easy-to-read brochure will reflect the organisation's professional approach to the conference and appeal to potential delegates.

Design

You may decide to design and produce the brochures yourself, using a desktop publishing program such as Microsoft Publisher. Alternatively, the conference committee may decide to engage a professional to design and prepare the brochures along with other stationery for the conference including the logo and the letterhead. On the other hand, the company may have its own art or design department capable of producing the required materials.

If it is decided to use an outside agency or designer, they must be given a clear brief and know exactly what is required in terms of size, style and content and the budget allocated for the work. Several quotes should be obtained before commissioning the work, as prices will vary between agencies.

Take into consideration the colour of the paper and inks to be used. If one of the registration options is to fax the completed registration form, make sure the colours chosen will not make it unreadable when sent. It may be best to stick with a separate white form or, if it is detachable from the rest of the brochure, the registration section should be a pale colour or white and printed in black ink.

Whether the brochure is being produced in-house or by an outside agency, the final draft should be checked and re-checked and proofread by at least one other person before it is printed.

Printing

As for the design aspect, several quotes should be obtained from suitable printers. The printer should be told the timeframe for production and when they can expect the camera-ready copy to be delivered to them. It may be a good idea to give the printer a deadline a week or two earlier than is necessary to allow for any unexpected delays.

Information to be included

The brochures/registration forms should contain the following information, if it is available at the time of mailing:

- title and theme of the conference;
- brief description of its nature or purpose;
- dates and location;
- speakers;
- topics;
- costs, and what is included in the price;
- other events, such as conference dinner, and costs;
- methods of payment;
- accommodation options (if applicable);
- discounted air fares available (if applicable);
- closing date for registration;
- payment method for overseas delegates (if applicable);
- email address and phone/fax numbers for enquiries; and
- the cancellations policy.

Information kits

As an alternative, a single mailing could include a form to be completed by the recipient, requesting further information or an information kit be sent to them. This would allow more lead time for arrangements to be confirmed before the information kits are prepared and printed, so they would contain a substantial amount of information about the conference, perhaps even a draft program and abstracts from speakers, and including a registration form.

Mailing list

The names collected on the registration list from the previous year's conference could be used as a basis for the mailing, or if the conference were one arranged for members of an association or professional body, then the mailing would be sent to all members and associate members as well.

Another way to reach possible delegates is through a cooperative mailing with another company that is targeting individuals with similar interests or in similar industry groups (sometimes called 'piggy-backing'). In this way, the cost of the mailing is shared and your brochures are sent to potential delegates you might not otherwise have reached.

Mailing lists can also be bought from various organisations such as chambers of commerce, publications and directories. Some of these lists can be tailored to a specific type of 'market', depending on the nature of the conference.

Other possible delegates

As registrations begin to flow in, an analysis of delegates' details could reveal another type of potential delegate. For example, if you discover the conference appeals to a large number of people in a particular kind of job, or in similar groups, you could arrange a mailing to individuals in these positions.

Internet

Notice of the conference could be posted on appropriate web sites. Alternatively, a conference web page could be designed and set up well in advance of the date of the conference. The web site would then be updated regularly as details were confirmed. A registration form should be added to the site at the appropriate time, as directed by the organising committee.

Professional publicist

If the allocated budget allows for it, a professional publicist could be hired to arrange the promotion of the conference, or to act as a consultant on certain aspects of the promotion, working with employees of the company or association arranging the conference.

EXERCISE 6

1. If the conference you were promoting was for members of a trade such as car manufacturers, in what ways could you promote the conference to potential target participants? Give four different methods you could use.

_____

_____

_____

_____

_____

_____

_____

_____

2. What is 'advertorial', what are its advantages, and why would it be of benefit to someone trying to reach a target market?

_____

_____

_____

3. If you were writing an article for a trade magazine about the conference, how should the 'copy' be presented?

_____

_____

_____

4. What other sorts of free promotion might you be able to arrange, apart from an article in a trade magazine?

_____

_____

_____

_____

_____

5. If you have sent out press releases to various newspapers, radio and TV stations, what should you do afterwards?

_____
_____
_____
_____
_____

6. What is an 'incentive' and how would you use one to encourage target participants to attend the conference?

_____
_____
_____
_____
_____

7. If you decided to produce a brochure to promote the conference, where could you find a list of target participants to send it to?

_____

_____

_____

_____

_____

_____

_____

_____

_____

8. If the promotional budget was rather generous, what could you do to make sure the publicity was organised professionally?

_____

_____

_____

_____

_____

_____

_____

_____

_____

_____

_____

3 Organise the conference

This element is concerned with the conference arrangements themselves and that they are made in accordance with the allocated lead times and budgets. Financial aspects such as requesting quotes for services are covered, and the fine detail of all the required arrangements are studied closely and explained in full.

Next, the process of recording acceptances and confirming registrations within the designated timelines is explained together with different methods of registering delegates. The special needs of some participants are considered in terms of the facilities provided by the chosen venue.

Confirmation of the program details including session times, excursions and the social program are discussed next as well as the final draft of the program and its contents. The dispatch of pre-conference information such as registration confirmations and details of travel and accommodation and any last minute changes are examined in the last unit of this element.

3.1 Conference arrangements are made in accordance with booking lead times and budget allocations

The arrangements that will need to be made in organising the conference may include some or all of the following:

- Booking the venue
- Hiring furniture
- Layout of room[s]
- Hiring and setting up equipment
- Catering
- Travel bookings
- Accommodation
- Provision of consumables
- Sponsorship
- Social program

*The word **protocol** is broadly defined as 'ceremonial etiquette', although its meaning has changed over the years. In the context of its usage here, protocol means 'the polite or correct way of doing something'.*

The arrangements required will depend very much on the type and size of the conference. The lead times required for bookings will vary between the different suppliers and will depend on their individual *protocols* and how busy they are. Needless to say, the earlier the bookings can be confirmed, the better.

Once the convener has confirmed the specific requirements for the conference, the process of making bookings can begin. This must be done as early as possible after the date, time and location of the conference have been confirmed and the total number of attendees is known, or can be estimated to as near as possible the expected final total.

Budget allocation

When making bookings for the venue, and other arrangements such as catering, it will be necessary to bear in mind the amount of money or budget that has been allocated for such expenditure.

There is little point in booking a fabulous venue with all kinds of bells and whistles, or engaging a brilliant caterer who produces exquisite foods, if their costs are way outside the allocated budget.

It is a good idea to have the total budget for the conference broken down into cost centres for each item, with certain limits or caps set on the amount that may be spent on each one. This will ease the task of checking that quotes for individual services are inside the guidelines, and assist in keeping track of the costs. For a more detailed discussion of budgeting, see pages 13 to 15.

Requesting quotations

Before any bookings are made and the deposits paid, it is usual business practice to approach at least two suppliers of each item to be arranged, and request they submit *quotations* for the cost. For example, the hiring of audio-visual equipment and setting it up at the venue, or the catering and serving of morning and afternoon teas.

The organisation's required procedures relating to the conference arrangements may *stipulate* that all quotations received should be in writing and submitted to the conference committee for their consideration and decision as to which supplier will be used. (It is not always best to choose the cheapest quote for the supply of an item if the quality or service is likely to be poor.)

The information given to the companies to provide the quotes must be as detailed as possible, as any omissions that come to light later—for example, extra equipment being needed because someone underestimated or miscounted the number of audio-visual set-ups required—will be added to the cost. This may, in turn, result in the budget being exceeded. That is another reason why a written quote is preferable, as there can be no misunderstandings later of what the actual service quoted on entailed.

*A **quotation** or **quote** is 'the statement of the current price of a commodity or service'.*

***Stipulate** means 'to make an express demand or arrangement, as the condition of agreement'; 'to specify'.*

Mining the archives

It is often extremely helpful to refer to the files which were compiled when previous conferences were arranged, if there were any previous conferences, and if such files exist. These files should provide most of the details and background information you need to make the arrangements, such as possible venues, the costs of various items and the suppliers chosen, the number of people the venues could hold comfortably, and details about the catering arrangements and names of caterers who were approached.

Alternatively, those who were responsible for making these arrangements in the past, or were part of a previous organising committee, may be able to provide valuable assistance.

Booking the venue

As pointed out in 1.2 *Conference Facilities Requirements...* on page 9, the conference may require only one meeting area. Alternatively, a large space for plenary sessions together with smaller meeting rooms for concurrent workshops and presentations may be required.

If there are no records from previous conferences, and noone in your company who can provide advice, you could contact a professional events management company who would be able to offer suggestions about suitable locations for you to consider, as well as the names of catering firms you might approach for quotes. It would be a simple matter, then, to contact the venue and ask them to send you their latest brochure, including any services they can provide, such as catering and equipment, and their scale of fees.

If the budget allows it, the events management team could take the organising off your hands and do all of it, or some of it, for you. It is well worth considering using a professional conference organiser if the event is complex, with much co-ordination involved, and spread over several days. It would certainly be time-efficient to hire a specialist to assist you, but may not be cost effective.

Hiring furniture

Most conference venues will provide any necessary furniture such as tables and chairs as part of the cost of the venue hire. However, if the conference is being arranged on the company's premises or at a location where extra chairs and/or tables will be required, the appropriate companies should be approached to quote on the supply, delivery and post-conference removal of the necessary furniture.

Some hire firms can supply individual desks such as those used in some secondary schools and college lecture theatres. These are ideal if delegates are not seated at tables but will be taking notes or need to have a surface on which to spread their papers while the conference is in progress.

Layout of room

As described earlier, the room layout will vary little, if at all, if the conference is restricted to one room for all sessions. How the furniture may be arranged for different types and purposes of conferences is covered in 1.2 *Conference Facilities Requirements...* under the sub-heading *Amenities and decor* on page 9.

Should the conference be organised in such a way that it provides concurrent sessions and/or workshops conducted in a number of small syndicate rooms, these may need to be set up differently to suit each session. The arrangement will depend on the format of the session and the presenter's requirements. For example: question-and-answer session with a panel seated at a long table and attendees facing; PowerPoint or flipchart presentation with attendees seated in rows, as in a theatre; 'round-table' discussion led by a speaker with participation of all in attendance. The chairs could be arranged in a large circle or several concentric circles.

Setting up the rooms

Staff of the venue, or some of the organisers would need to set up or rearrange each room according to the presentation and in liaison with the presenter or chairperson of each session. Also to be considered is whether any tables are required for equipment such as audio-visual or overhead projectors, and screens, flipcharts, and so on.

When the program for the conference is in its final draft form, with the speakers confirmed, the meeting rooms should be allocated for each of the sessions. Any requirements such as those just described will have been advised by the speakers and noted, and arrangements made for the rooms to be set up appropriately and in good time for each session.

Running sheets for set-ups

It would be necessary to provide the people responsible for setting up equipment in the rooms and/or arranging the furniture, with a running sheet for each day. The sheet would show the day, time and room allocated for each session along with details of the set-up and any necessary equipment. For example:

WILDLIFE IN THE SUBURBS CONFERENCE DAY TWO: Tuesday, May 23			
TIME	ROOM	PRESENTER	REQUIREMENTS
9.00	Wattle	**David Suzuki** *Endangered or Extinct?*	Microphone Lectern Chairs in rows
10.30	Banksia	**Jasper Pik** *Bugs and Other Critters*	OHP Screen Chairs in rows
10.30	Wattle	**Jenny Green** *What Are the Options for Preservation?*	Chairs in circle (round table discussion)

Hiring and setting up equipment

Some or all of the following may be required for a conference:

- audio-visual equipment
- computer equipment
- electronic whiteboards
- microphones
- teleconferencing equipment
- flip charts
- overhead projectors and screens
- tape recorders
- videoconferencing monitors and video cams
- large overhead screen or monitors

One of the conference committee's tasks will be to confirm what equipment, if any, will be required by each of the speakers and presenters and compile a complete list so that quotes for hiring it can be requested. The venue you book may have some or all of the necessary equipment for hire. However, if the conference venue is not able to supply some or any of the equipment and set it up, then outside companies should be approached for quotes for performing the task. The management of the conference venue should be able to recommend several hire companies that could arrange for the equipment to be delivered and set up.

Catering

This topic has been considered in 1.2 *Conference Facilities Requirements*...on page 12, and it may be worth revisiting at this point. Again, the files compiled for previous conferences would be invaluable in providing guidance about the catering arrangements required and the names of caterers to approach.

The type of catering required will depend very much on: the budget; the number of attendees; the location; any *precedents* from past conferences; the requirements of the convener.

*A **precedent** is 'a previous occurrence used to justify taking the same action in later, similar situations'.*

The catering may simply be the provision of a variety of teas, coffee, biscuits and cakes set out appropriately for the size of the gathering at the morning and afternoon tea breaks, and a lunch for attendees, if the conference is a one-day affair. Whether the lunch is a simple meal such as sandwiches and fruit, a buffet, or a sit-down luncheon with several courses would be decided by the conference committee.

If a welcome party is planned for the eve of the conference, then the type of drinks to be served and/or available at the bar and whether any finger food, canapés or 'nibblies' are to be provided should be discussed, costed and confirmed with the chosen caterers. Consideration should also be given to the possibility of hiring staff to serve drinks and food at the party. Budget limitations should be kept in mind when making these arrangements.

The menu and wines for the conference dinner will also need to be finalised and ordered, based on the number of delegates who have paid and registered to attend. If the conference is to be held at a conference centre or a hotel which specialises in conferences, the management should be able to take care of all the catering arrangements necessary for the various functions, and provide the staff.

Travel bookings

If invited keynote or guest speakers will be traveling from interstate or overseas to attend the conference, the organisers may have agreed to *subsidise* the cost of their air fares either in part or in total. The bookings may be made by the speakers or by the organisation, and if it is the organisation's responsibility to do this, then dates and preferred times should be confirmed with the speakers before any bookings are made.

If the conference is being held at a distance from the head office of a company, arrangements should be made for the transportation of staff members who will attend. This may be by car or aircraft, depending on the distance and location.

Accommodation

Again, accommodation for keynote and guest speakers may be paid for by the conference organisers. Before bookings are made, any special requirements with regard to the type or location of the accommodation of those concerned should be *ascertained*. Accommodation for staff of an organisation would be arranged in line with the usual company procedures or under the direction of the conference committee.

Provision of consumables

As discussed earlier, if special conference **stationery** is to be prepared and printed, the design and logo should be finalised very early in the planning so the stationery can be used in all correspondence *pertaining* to the conference.

Final copy for the conference **dinner menus**, any **signage** and the book of **abstracts** of speakers' presentations should all be ready to be printed four weeks before the conference. If these materials are being produced in-house, a shorter lead time could be applied.

If **satchels** are being provided for delegates, these should also be ordered six to eight weeks in advance. If a sponsor is providing the satchels, the required number should be conveyed to the person responsible for ordering them as soon as it is confirmed. Artwork for the overprinting of the satchels should be approved by the conference committee and the sponsor in good time.

If it is planned to provide **pads** and **pens**, these should be ordered promptly after the number of delegates is known. The pads should be overprinted with the conference name and logo or that of the sponsor, if this has been arranged. Again, approval of the artwork needs to be secured before printing.

Name tags should be printed in the week before the conference. These could be produced in-house or professionally printed with the conference logo and delegate name included. Alternatively, staff could write the delegates' names on cards printed with the conference logo and insert them into tag holders.

As discussed on page 68 under *Computerised Registration Systems*, some software packages will print out name tags as registrations are recorded, so if this method is used, only **tag holders** will need to be ordered so the name tags can be inserted into them.

Whatever the chosen method, the type used for names should be large and in bold so it can be read at a reasonable distance. In this way, delegates will avoid causing themselves and others embarrassment by peering at other delegates' chests to find out who they are and where they come from.

The final copy for the **program** should be ready for the printer four weeks before the conference date, or less, if the production is in-house. It is wise to wait for as long as possible before printing the program, because there are often last-minute changes or cancellations to be dealt with.

NB: When ordering consumables, it is advisable to allow approximately 15 percent extra conference satchels and their contents, and blank name tags for late registrations.

Sponsorship

If the conference committee has decided to invite suitable companies to mount a display as part of the conference (as described on page 4 under the heading *Purposes and required outcomes for convening a conference*), and to sponsor some aspects of the conference such as providing the satchels for delegates, paying for the printing of the dinner menu, or subsidising the catering, the companies concerned should be given six months' notice.

It is usually the custom to print in the conference program a full list of the companies participating in the trade display, with special mentions given to those that have sponsored some part of the conference as described above. Should a company sponsor an event, such as the welcoming party for delegates, the name of the company should be prominently displayed at the function. Companies are usually able to supply their own sign for this eventuality.

If some companies are providing brochures or catalogues to be inserted into the delegates' satchels (for a fee), the number of attendees will need to be confirmed with the companies concerned, as well as the location for delivery of the material for packing into the satchels.

Social program

The social program, particularly any planned excursions for delegates and their partners, should be booked as soon as its nature and cost have been decided. The numbers participating would be confirmed when they are known. This would also apply to any accompanying persons activities such as guided tours.

EXERCISE 7

1. If you were given the task of making the conference arrangements and bookings, what things would you need to be sure of before you began? Name six.

_____

_____

_____

_____

_____

_____

2. Explain why you should make and confirm bookings as early as possible.

_____

_____

_____

3. How could you go about estimating the expected total number of attendees so that arrangements could be made for items such as catering and printing programs for the delegates' satchels?

_____

_____

_____

_____

_____

_____

4. What is another word that means 'stipulate'?

_____

5. Give two reasons why it would be a good idea to have the total budget for the conference broken down into cost centres.

_____

_____

_____

_____

_____

_____

6. Give two reasons why it would be important to request written quotes from providers of services.

_____

_____

_____

_____

_____

_____

7. Give two examples, apart from those in the text, of the way a room could be set up for a small session or workshop.

_____

_____

_____

_____

_____

8. Name four things to be considered when organising catering for a conference.

_____

_____

_____

_____

_____

_____

_____

_____

_____

9. Explain the difference between 'time-efficient' and 'cost- effective'.

_____

_____

_____

_____

_____

_____

_____

_____

_____

10. What is a concurrent session?

_____

_____

_____

11. How would you set up a room for a question-and-answer session?

_____

_____

_____

_____

12. If it was your job to set up the Banksia Room for the 10.30 am session for Jenny Green at the 'Wildlife in the Suburbs' conference, how would you know how to arrange the furniture and what equipment may be required?

_____

_____

_____

_____

13. In what circumstances would you need to order only name-tag holders and not name tags as well?

_____

_____

_____

14. Why would the design and logo for the conference be one of the first things to be organised?

_____

_____

_____

_____

3.2 Acceptances recorded, fees receipted and participants confirmed

As the registration forms come in, the names should be recorded in alphabetical order and receipts issued. If delegates are registering for other events such as a pre-conference party or the conference dinner, these details should be noted as well. An efficient way to do this would be to prepare different sheets to record the various items, so each is kept separate and the total number attending each event may be easily found.

So, there could be several different registration lists with headings such as:

- Conference
- Pre-conference party
- Excursion
- Conference dinner

Dates of registration should be monitored carefully if an 'early bird' registration offer has been made, to ensure the correct amount has been filled in on the registration form and paid by cheque or credit card, both before and after the cut-off date for the early bird offer.

Other variations in fees may include special rates for members, non-members and students, where applicable, so those recording the registrations and issuing receipts should be aware of these different scales of fees.

All credit card payments will need to be processed according to the organisation's normal practice.

Computerised registration systems

Software packages that have been specifically designed to streamline the registration process for conferences are now available. By keying in a delegate's name you can produce:

- A personalised letter of confirmation
- A receipt
- A name tag
- Allocate hotel bookings, workshops etc.

There is a growing number of software packages with different benefits. For example, modules can be incorporated to plan and track catering, accommodation, partner programs and excursions. Most of these programs can be networked so others involved in planning and organising the conference can access and use the system. This sort of application has great administration and time-saving potential, but can be expensive.

Receipts and confirmation details

Receipts should be posted to delegates to acknowledge their payment of the conference fees. The receipts should itemise any other payments made as well, such as the fee for an excursion or conference dinner. Each receipt could be accompanied by a letter confirming the date, time and location of the conference (see page 73) and other information such as availability of parking or public transport, instructions on where to go on arrival, a reminder of the registration time and a map of the venue.

If workshop preferences have been allocated at this stage, the time and location of these should also be advised.

However, it may be planned to provide a set of speakers' abstracts to delegates before the conference so they are able to gain information about the different sessions or workshops available and so make selections that are relevant or of particular interest to them. In this case, the receipts and letters could be set aside until the abstracts are printed so that only one mailing is necessary.

Number of participants confirmed

Once registrations have closed, the committee should be informed immediately of the total number of participants for each event. The numbers can then be conveyed to those responsible for confirming:

- the catering for morning and afternoon teas;
- the hiring of chairs and tables;
- set up and catering for the conference dinner;
- the number of conference dinner menus to be printed;
- numbers booked for the excursion; and
- the number of delegates' satchels and other consumables required.

Registration records

It would be useful to keep all the processed registration forms in an alphabetical file at the registration desk to ensure that, should the need arise, any particular delegate's queries may be quickly checked.

3.3 Participants' special needs identified

At the time of considering suitable venues, the possibility of some delegates with special needs attending should be taken into consideration. The following checklist should be compiled and each question investigated before a venue can be considered to be suitable:

- Are there points of access and facilities for people with disabilities?
- Are disabled toilets within reasonable distance of the conference room(s)?
- If the conference room(s) is not on the ground floor, is there a suitably-sized lift to transport anyone in a wheelchair to and from sessions?
- Are the caterers able to supply food for diabetics and other special dietary requirements such as gluten-free biscuits to be served at morning and afternoon coffee breaks?
- Will the caterers provide meals for vegetarians and vegans on request?
- Is there a hearing-loop system for any delegates who may have hearing difficulties?
- Are services available for delegates with a sight disability?

There may be other specific needs not listed above that you know about which should also be considered and catered for at the conference.

3.4 Program details confirmed and conference papers prepared

As the date of the conference draws closer, arrangements are firmed up and registrations begin to flow in, the details of the conference program should be confirmed so that the final draft can be prepared for printing.

Timing of sessions

If a number of different rooms will be used for concurrent sessions, you should make sure enough time has been built into each day's program to allow delegates to move between rooms. This extra time would be particularly important if some sessions are to take place on different floors of the venue, as is sometimes the case. This will avoid delegates walking in late for sessions, which can be very disruptive to the speaker as well as to the listeners.

Check and recheck

A letter of confirmation containing the title of their presentation or session and the day and time it is to be given should have been sent to all presenters and keynote speakers some weeks before, and the attendance of any official guests should also have been confirmed.

However it may be advisable to check the files or ask the person responsible for this aspect of the arrangements to ensure that nothing and noone has been overlooked. The details contained in these letters of confirmation can be used to compile or check the final draft program to make sure they match in every respect, including spelling of names, and that there are no omissions.

Excursion details

If an excursion or excursions have been arranged, the arrangements, times and other details should be confirmed with the provider or the tour guide to ensure there are no misunderstandings. Only then should the relevant information be added to the program on the page for that day's activities.

Social program

Details of the social events should also be added to the program in the appropriate places. For example, a welcome cocktail party and the conference dinner. All details such as times and venue must be checked before they are entered into the final draft of the program.

Final draft program

At some point during the organising of the conference, it may have been necessary to rearrange the order of some sessions or to find alternative speakers, so it is a good idea to meticulously check every item line by line to ensure the program is 100 per cent accurate. In particular, attention should be paid to checking that the following are correct in every respect:

❑ Headings.

❑ Day and date on each page.

❑ Beginning and ending times of every session.

❑ Beginning/ending times of morning and afternoon teas and lunch.

❑ Names of speaker(s) and moderator for each session (right names and spelt correctly).

❑ Titles of sessions.

❑ Identification numbers of sessions (if several are running concurrently).

- ❑ Rooms where sessions are to be held (if rooms have been allocated at this point).

- ❑ Abstracts are correctly cross-referenced to session identification numbers and their titles and authors match those in the list of sessions and in the program list.

- ❑ List of sponsors and their logos.

- ❑ List of exhibitors (if applicable).

- ❑ Any maps are legible, correctly orientated and clearly labeled.

- ❑ Page numbers of the program.

- ❑ Running heads and/or running bottoms on the program pages.

Above all, the spelling must be checked and rechecked, preferably by more than one person. It is a well-known rule in publishing that the writer of something should not proofread it; because of their familiarity with the material, they tend to have blind spots when it comes to spotting errors in spelling and grammar

3.5 Pre-conference information is dispatched within designated timelines

As discussed on page 70, a receipt for fees paid for registration should be posted to each delegate once the registration procedure has been completed. The receipt should be accompanied by a letter of confirmation setting out the date, time and location of the conference, together with other information such as accommodation bookings made (where requested) and reservations for the conference dinner. A sample of such a letter appears on the following page.

Dear …………

Thank you for registering for this year's conference as a residential participant at the Nikko. The organising committee is confident all delegates will find our program beneficial and provide you with the opportunity to meet and interact with colleagues from a wide spectrum of your industry.

Updates on conference information can be found at www.magger.nsw.au. Information regarding your participation at the conference follows.

Please contact me if the details need correction or if you have any enquiries.

James Redox

On behalf of the Conference Committee

Accommodation: Share with person to be advised at registration.
Occupy room: Thursday 6th after 3pm
Vacate room: Saturday 8th before 10am.

Fees paid for conference, accommodation, conference dinner and excursion.

GENERAL INFORMATION

° The first formal conference session begins at 8.30 am on Thursday 6th.
° Breakfast and lunches are served in dining areas. Room service is at your expense.
° Parking is available at the hotel at $16.50 a day (conference rate).
° Concurrent sessions selections—options will be displayed at registration desk for delegates to nominate their choices.
° Excursion coach departs 8.30am Friday 7th. Meet in the foyer.

For delegates arriving prior to and including Wednesday 5th:
° Register at the hotel reception desk.
° Register for the conference and pre-conference activities at the conference reception suite on 2nd floor. (The suite will be open from 11am until 9pm on Wednesday 5th.)

For delegates arriving on Thursday 6th:
° Register at the hotel reception desk.
° Register for the conference at the registration desk on the main conference floor from 7.30am. Coffee will be available.

Cancellations:
28 days—full refund; 7–27 days—50 percent refund; 6 days—no refund.

Enquiries phone: (02) 9933 5678

Details of travel and accommodation

While a booking for accommodation may be confirmed in the letter as indicated in the previous example, it may also be helpful to enclose a map showing the location of the conference venue and the hotel—if it is separate from the conference area, and indicate entrances to both.

It would also be helpful to include on a separate sheet, information about public transport and parking availability. For example:

> Parking is available in parking stations in and around the conference venue. Public transport is also available to the venue. There is little on-street parking available and parking restrictions exist. Please park with care and check signage. The Convener will not be liable for any parking infringements.

If airline or train bookings have been made at a special discounted conference rate, vouchers or documentation for this should also be enclosed with the letter and receipt.

Floor plan of venue

If a number of areas separate from the main hall (where the plenary sessions will be held) have been allocated for workshops and other functions, it would be appropriate to include a floor plan of the conference venue showing the location of these rooms.

The registration desk, cocktail party area, dining room and toilet areas should also be marked, and the exhibition area, if a display or trade fair is to be part of the conference. This will allow delegates to familiarise themselves with the layout before arriving at the conference. Venues can usually supply maps or floor plans so they can be copied and distributed to delegates.

Speakers' abstracts

Pre-reading material such as the speakers' abstracts and biographical details should be provided at this time as well. This will allow delegates to gain background information about the different speakers, sessions and workshops, to help them to select the ones which would be most beneficial or interesting for them.

If the abstracts are to be printed and bound as a single volume separate from the program, it, too, should be checked and proofread for errors or omissions. In particular, the cross-referencing of dates, times and session numbers should be double-checked with those in the program. The front cover should show the conference logo, the title, dates and location of the conference as well as the names of key sponsors at the bottom, such as: 'Conference proudly sponsored by Optus'.

Changes to the conference program

If any changes have been made to the program as it was originally promoted and described in the advertising or mail-outs, a separate sheet of paper drawing delegates' attention to these changes should be included inside the front cover of the program before it is sent to delegates.

EXERCISE 8

1. Describe, in your own words, how you would organise the task of recording acceptances and keeping track of which delegates had registered for some or all of the social activities at a conference.

_____

_____

_____

_____

_____

_____

_____

_____

2. Give four reasons why there may be a variation in the fees paid for the conference.

_____

_____

_____

_____

_____

_____

_____

_____

3. List six arrangements for a conference that could not be confirmed with the providers of the services until the total number of delegates was known.

_____

_____

_____

_____

_____

_____

4. What is one arrangement conference organisers could make to try to ensure that delegates attending concurrent sessions do not disrupt a presentation by walking in after a session has begun?

_____

_____

_____

_____

_____

5. Give six examples of why the final draft program has to be checked so meticulously, i.e. the types of errors that may occur.

_____

_____

_____

_____

_____

_____

_____

_____

_____

_____

_____

6. Why is it emphasised that more than one person should proofread the final draft program?

_____

_____

_____

_____

7. If any changes were made to the program after it has been printed but before it is mailed out to participants, how would you let delegates know about them?

_____

_____

_____

_____

8. If you had registered for the conference to be held at The Nikko at Darling Harbour, and decided to book in at the hotel on Tuesday 4th, where and when could you register for the conference and pre-conference activities?

_____

_____

_____

_____

_____

_____

9. What is the importance of sending speakers' abstracts and biographical details to delegates before the conference?

_____

_____

_____

_____

_____

_____

4 Co-ordinate conference proceedings

This fourth element focuses on the activities of the final few days preceding the conference and the administration requirements during the conference.

In the first unit we consider all the arrangements that have made and the confirmation and checks required to ensure all will go according to plan.

Second, the process of registering delegates as they arrive is explained and options for dealing with a large number of delegates and other contingencies, such as late payments, are suggested.

Should changes to the published program be made, the protocols for dealing with this are explored, followed by options that might be available should the venue suddenly become unavailable. Lesser problems that could arise during the conference are also dealt with here.

Next, a discussion of the management of speakers and their requirements is provided and finally the administrative requirements including financial matters and keeping records are addressed. This is followed by a discussion of the duties of chairpersons and moderators during the conference.

4.1 Conference facilities are checked to confirm they meet agreed requirements

In the week or so before the conference, it would be wise to make a final check of all the facilities and to confirm that all outside suppliers are prepared to meet the prearranged requirements of the organisers.

As a result:

❑ You will know the size and location of the room or rooms that have been reserved at the conference venue, and know that they contain an adequate number of power points and phone lines.

❑ You will have a list of the rooms allocated for sessions and workshops and will have confirmed the approximate number of seats and the different seating arrangements required for these sessions, and any extra furniture that will be needed.

❑ The running sheets for staff or helpers who will rearrange the rooms and set up equipment for different sessions will have been checked and cross-referenced to the room allocation list to make sure they match up. These lists will show any equipment needed, including microphones, for each session. Sufficient copies of the sheets will have been made for the organisers as well as for those actually performing the tasks. These people will have been briefed as to the conference committee requirements.

❑ If special lighting effects have been requested, or a light is to be added to the speakers' lectern, you will know that this has been arranged.

❑ A quick call to the suppliers of any electronic or audio-visual equipment that has been booked will confirm that all will be delivered and set up according to instructions, and in good time. Also any flip charts, whiteboards and so on. (Some of this equipment may be supplied by the venue management.) Once the equipment has been delivered and set up, it must be checked and rechecked to ensure that it works properly. Any PowerPoint presentations should be loaded and tested, if that is possible.

❑ If there is an inbuilt sound system at the venue, you will have checked that it functions correctly and has good volume control.

❑ Arrangements are in place to cater for any delegates with disabilities or special needs.

❑ You will know that the caterers are clear on the numbers they are providing for, the areas where they are to serve morning and afternoon tea and other meals, if these have been arranged. Also that they have noted any special dietary requirements of delegates and/or speakers.

❑ You will know that any decorations, flowers, place cards or signage will be delivered and set up at the welcoming cocktail party and the conference dinner before guests begin to arrive. Beverages will be provided as ordered.

❑ You will know that the agreed menus for the conference dinner will be provided as agreed and that any special meals or requirements of delegates have been noted. Also that the correct wines and table waters have been ordered or delivered.

❑ You will know that enough tables and chairs will be supplied for those working in the registration area and that space will be provided for reference files, delegates' name tags (arranged in alphabetical order) and satchels. A large noticeboard will be available for displaying session options, announcements about any extra activities, delegates' messages, a floor plan or map and other information appropriate for delegates.

❑ If payments for late registrations or social events such as the conference dinner will be accepted using credit cards, you will have confirmed that a phone line will be provided for the credit card facility.

❏ You will know that the registration area will be clearly marked with signs at the entrance to the area, and the location will be shown at the entrance to the venue itself.

❏ You will know that signs directing delegates to session rooms will be provided and set up on the day.

❏ You will know that tea and coffee will be provided for delegates in the registration area on the first morning of the conference, if this has been arranged.

❏ If discounted conference accommodation is part of the conference package, you will have confirmed that the rooms have been allocated.

❏ You will know that accommodation for speakers has been allocated by the hotel.

❏ You will know that, if an affiliated trade fair or exhibition is to be mounted, the area has been prepared appropriately and the spaces for exhibitors marked out, numbered and labeled for ease of identification by representatives of the companies involved.

4.2 Participants are registered in accordance with planned registration procedures

As participants arrive to register for the conference, their names will need to be checked off on a prepared list of participants and a name tag issued, along with a satchel or information kit. The method used to do this efficiently and quickly is simple. At one table, delegates register and are issued with their name tag, then they move on to the next table where they are handed their conference satchel or kit.

Registration period

If the advertised registration period is too short, say 15 minutes for 150 delegates, the desks will be overwhelmed with participants because most will arrive at the same time. However if there is a longer registration period—say, 45 minutes or more—delegates will tend to arrive at intervals throughout the period, so there will be less pressure on the registration officers and shorter queues for the delegates.

Registering a large group of delegates

Depending on the number of delegates, more than one person may be required at each desk to process the throng of people quickly. In this case, the list of participants could be broken down into several alphabetical groupings, much like the method used at polling booths.

So, for example, one registrar would have names beginning with A-J, the next would have K-S and the third would have T-Z. It would be wise to indicate this at the desk with signs showing the alphabetical groupings, so delegates can arrange themselves accordingly.

Name tags

At some conferences—usually small ones—name tags are laid out on the registration desk in alphabetical order so they are easy to locate. However, for security reasons this method may not be desirable, in which case the name tags will be arranged alphabetically in a file or box to be handed to delegates by the registration officers. This precludes any *interloper* or unregistered person taking the badge of someone who has pre-registered, and just walking in.

*An **interloper** is 'someone who intrudes without proper authority'.*

Late payments

Some delegates may wish to book and pay for other activities such as the conference dinner or an excursion when they arrive at the venue, and if so, this could be done at a third table so registrations are not delayed and delegates who have pre-paid are processed quickly. This third desk could also be used for any late registrations and queries. If a credit card facility will be provided for payments, a phone line should be available at the desk.

Signage

Each desk should be clearly marked so that delegates do not become disoriented. Signs could read:

PRE-PAID REGISTRATIONS
CONFERENCE SATCHELS
LATE PAYMENTS AND ENQUIRIES

Creating a welcoming atmosphere

Staff who will be registering participants as they arrive should make delegates feel welcome and comfortable. The provision of tea or coffee in the registration area helps newcomers relax and also provides a networking environment for delegates.

Most venues include refreshments on arrival for conference delegates as part of the service they provide, but it may be wise to check. If not, make sure it is ordered when making the other catering arrangements, and add it to the budget.

Briefing staff

Make sure all personnel manning the registration desks are carefully briefed in relation to all aspects of the conference. Each person should have a copy of the program showing the times of each session, the speakers, and a map showing locations of rooms. They should also be able to direct delegates to the session rooms and know the location of facilities such as toilets, coffee shops and dining rooms.

4.3 Any late changes to the published program are communicated to participants

If there are any changes to the published program after it has been printed and inserted into the delegates' satchels, the details of the alterations should be printed out and distributed to delegates on registration.

Changes after registration

If the changes are made after delegates have registered, copies of the notice of alteration should be placed in a prominent position where delegates are likely to see them—on tables where the morning or afternoon teas are served, for example.

A copy of the changes should also be placed on the noticeboard adjacent to the conference enquiries desk. The chairperson should announce the changes at the following sessions and ask delegates to pick up a copy of the sheet at the next break or make a note of the changes on their own programs.

If the change is made after the first day of the conference, the chairperson should make an announcement at the next morning's keynote address or plenary session, where all delegates are likely to be in attendance, outlining the change or changes to the published program and asking delegates to make a note of them.

4.4 Contingency arrangements are made to ensure the smooth running of the conference

Should your worst nightmare come to pass—for example, the hotel or venue is damaged in a violent storm, or there is a strike by staff or transport workers—it may be decided to abandon the conference altogether, or seek an alternative venue.

*A **contingency** is 'an unforeseen or unknown future event or condition'.*

Alternative venues

If the conference committee or management of the organisation considered it appropriate, and if sufficient time were available, an alternative venue may be found for the conference. The files containing the names of possible venues, which was compiled at the beginning of the planning phase, should be consulted to see if another suitable venue is available at short notice.

If the conference was small, or one arranged by the organisation for its staff members and associates, it would not be such a big problem. However, in the case of a larger conference, particularly one open to delegates from a variety of organisations and locations, it would be more problematic, and a change to the venue could only happen early in the planning stages before advertising and mailings had been prepared and printed.

On the other hand, if it was imperative that the venue or dates had to be changed, then fresh mailings and advertisements would need to be prepared and sent out. It would also mean that the catering and other arrangements would be affected and could involve major reorganisation and much expense.

Lesser problems

Should lesser problems befall the conference arrangements, such as the caterers or audio visual suppliers being unable to meet their obligations, alternative suppliers should be contacted immediately and their urgent assistance requested. This will obviously affect the smooth running of the conference, but it is best to continue with less than perfect arrangements and facilities rather than abandon the whole thing entirely.

If it is merely a matter of a speaker getting lost or overlooking their commitment, or the PowerPoint presentation refusing to function, it is best to seek assistance or try to work around the problem rather than delay or cancel a session while waiting for a remedy to arrive.

If the equipment fails, most good speakers should be able to improvise and give an amended presentation rather than feel obliged to cancel their session. It may also be possible to swap one session for another, if that is a practical solution to the problem.

Contingency arrangements

It is wise to have contingency arrangements in place before the conference begins, such as a list of alternative suppliers, should any need to be contacted for assistance. Similarly, if it is practical to do so, a list of alternative speakers who may be available at short notice could be compiled together with their contact details. The name, address and phone number of the nearest instant printing shop should also be added to the file in case extra sets of documents are required urgently.

All this information should be kept in a Troubleshooting File with phone, fax and mobile numbers of the companies or their representatives. As well, a list of companies that can supply emergency assistance or back-up equipment such as:

- audio-visual equipment;
- audio-visual technicians;
- computer technicians;
- sound equipment;
- electricians; and
- caterers.

The venue's management should be able to help in some circumstances, so it would be best to ask them for assistance or advice first in the case of a problem.

Extra staff

If extra staff members will be required to help with registrations or other matters to do with the conference, other selected employees of the company should be on call so that they can fill in immediately should someone who was rostered to assist becomes ill or is unavoidably detained.

4.5 Speakers' schedules are managed and their conference requirements met

Ensure all speakers have been provided with the necessary information so they will be able to arrive in good time for their presentations. Set out the following in the letter of confirmation:

- ❑ Date and time of the presentation.

- ❑ Its title.

- ❑ The room where it will be given.

- ❑ The phone number and address of the venue.

- ❑ Instructions on how to get there by public transport and the availability and location of parking stations.

- ❑ Details of how to find the conference rooms at the venue.

- ❑ The name of a contact person to speak to on arrival.

Other guidelines such as the following could be included in the letter:

To ensure the conference flows smoothly and maintains the schedule shown in the program, the committee is seeking co-operation of all speakers to follow the guidelines below.

If possible, please rehearse your presentation to ensure that it will fit into the time allocated. If you intend taking questions from delegates, make allowance for that within the time allotted for your session. We suggest you allow yourself enough time to prepare any visual aids you will use and to familiarise yourself with the equipment provided before your session.

If the conference organisers are providing accommodation, the specific details should be included in the letter. For example:

The Conference Committee has arranged overnight accommodation for you at the Hyatt Hotel in Park Street. This includes a continental breakfast served in your suite. As agreed, you will be responsible for any other costs in relation to your stay.

If the accommodation is at a different venue to the conference, a map should be included with the letter showing the quickest route from the hotel to the conference.

Time of arrival

It would be useful for the organisers or the person responsible for managing the speakers' schedules to find out and note the approximate time each speaker intends to arrive at the venue. It would then be possible for a representative of the committee to meet them as they arrive.

Some presenters may be unable to attend the whole conference, and may come simply to give their talk and then leave. In such circumstances, it would save undue concern if this information were known and written on the organiser's schedule for easy reference.

Speakers' room

If it is considered appropriate, and the budget allows it, it can be helpful to set aside or book a room exclusively for the use of speakers. Here they can prepare for or rest between sessions in privacy, have a coffee or cool drink and collect themselves before a presentation.

Chairpersons and moderators

On the first day of the conference, or several days before the conference begins, the session chairpersons and workshop leaders should be given information packs containing the relevant conference papers and the abstracts and biographies of the speakers. If it is possible, the moderators and speakers should be introduced before their sessions.

Conference equipment and room arrangements

As described on pages 59-60, all equipment requirements and layout of rooms for speakers will have been noted and organised.

It may be of assistance to introduce each presenter to the visual aids technician or operator so that any details can be discussed before their session. Jugs of fresh water and glasses should be available in each room for the chairperson and the speaker.

Microphones

If microphones are necessary for some presentations, find out what type the speakers would prefer to use. If reading from notes at a lectern, a speaker may prefer to use the microphone attached to the stand, while others may prefer to use a radio mike attached to their clothing. This is useful if the speaker is using a flip chart or whiteboard or tends to move around the platform during their talk. Another option is a roving or cordless mike which can be handed to delegates to ask questions at the end of a presentation. Some speakers prefer to use this type of microphone themselves, as well.

Equipment management

Audio-visual assistance should be available at all times throughout the sessions to assist if there are any problems or breakdowns and to help speakers with their presentations. This assistance could be provided by a professional technician hired independently for the duration of the conference, or provided by the company from which the equipment has been hired.

The technician should also be able to provide small replacement items such as spare batteries or bulbs, should the need arise.

4.6 Administration requirements are managed in accordance with conference plan/schedule

If any cash is taken by the official registrars for conference dinner bookings, late registrations, excursions and other events, precautions should be taken to ensure the cash box is safe at all times. If large amounts of money are accumulated, the venue management may be able to provide facilities to store it for a few hours in a safe or a lockable office area so it can be collected at the end of the day and banked.

These arrangements should be made before the beginning of the conference so there is no confusion about how the cash will be handled and to satisfy the organisers that the money will be secured appropriately.

Keeping records

All copies of receipts and credit card dockets issued to delegates should be set aside carefully. If time allows, a list of the cash items could be compiled and entered under headings such as *Registration*, *Dinner*, *Excursion*, etc. and kept in a file for later transfer to the accountant or accounts department of the organisation along with the receipts.

Should some delegates who have paid fail to attend the conference, their names should be recorded and kept in the conference files.

Organisers' checklists

If checklists have been prepared for those involved in implementing different aspects of the conference, these should be used and monitored to ensure everything has been done according to the conference plan and administration requirements, and that nothing has been overlooked.

There will be a variety of different checklists required, depending on the planning stage of the conference and the particular aspect or aspects that are being dealt with. For example, different checklists will apply to those actually at the conference venue helping with the administration, registration, speakers' schedules and so on.

The co-ordination of a large conference takes great skill and attention to all the tiny details, and checklists are essential tools for all personnel involved. Once a checklist is completed it should be signed off and dated and then filed for future reference.

Duties of chairpersons and moderators

As well as announcing each session, introducing the speaker and moderating the session, the chairperson or moderator should also ensure each speaker keeps to their allotted time and does not run over the scheduled period of their presentation. The chairperson will sometimes sum up after the talk, particularly if it is that of a keynote speaker, and request questions from the audience to the speaker or panel of speakers, if that is the agreed format of the session.

Announcing breaks

When a break is due for morning or afternoon tea or lunch, the chairperson will announce this and the duration of the break as well as the time when the conference proceedings will resume.

If an exhibition or trade show has been arranged, the chairperson should regularly remind delegates to visit it, particularly at the lunch break and after the formal part of the conference has finished for the day, or in the morning before sessions begin. It is important exhibitors feel they are getting their money's worth in terms of delegates' visits and exposure to their products.

Housekeeping

Another duty of the chairperson is to read out so-called 'housekeeping' notices concerning any changes to the program or other announcements which concern delegates such as requesting them to turn off their mobile phones whist the conference is in session.

Closing the conference

At the end of the conference, the chairperson should move a vote of thanks to all concerned: visitors, speakers, keynote speakers, sponsors and exhibitors.

Other administrative requirements

One registration desk should remain 'open' throughout the conference. Its function after the registration period is over would be to answer delegates' questions, provide tourist or sightseeing information, direct delegates to the locations of rooms as well as facilities such as the dining room or the toilets. There should be up-to-date copies of the conference program, maps of the venue and other conference papers available for any delegates who require a fresh or duplicate set. As well, extra copies of the evaluation questionnaire should be available with pens and a box for returning the completed forms.

Other helpful information to keep at the desk would be contact numbers for taxi services, the railway enquiry office and airlines. It goes without saying that the area will be kept neat and tidy at all times.

Signage

If the conference is being held at a university campus where some sessions are to be conducted in different buildings, signs should be set up at strategic points to direct delegates between sessions and to the catering areas and other facilities. If the conference is of several days' duration, someone should be assigned to check that the signs remain in place and legible despite any adverse weather conditions.

Assistance at sessions

If a roving microphone is to be used for delegates to ask questions at some sessions, arrangements should be made to ensure a member of the conference committee or a staff member will be available to perform this duty.

All personnel manning the registration desks and otherwise assisting at the conference should wear identity tags or badges.

EXERCISE 9

1. When delegates arrive on the first morning of a very large conference, describe the required steps for registration.

_____

_____

_____

_____

_____

2. What is the reasoning behind deciding to have a registration period of 45 minutes rather than 15 minutes?

_____

_____

_____

3. For what reasons would the name tags for delegates not be set out on a table for easy identification?

_____

_____

_____

4. List the three uses a third registration desk would provide on the first morning. What other equipment would this desk require?

_____

_____

_____

5. Apart from providing a welcoming atmosphere and refreshment on arrival, what other activity could the provision of tea and coffee bring about?

_____

_____

_____

6. Why would it be important to brief the personnel manning the registration desks?

_____

_____

_____

7. If there were some late changes to the published program, describe the methods you would use to make sure all delegates know of these changes.

_____

_____

_____

_____

8. If, due to unforeseen circumstances, the venue suddenly could not accommodate the conference you had arranged, what would be the first step you would take to find another suitable venue?

_____

_____

_____

9. In your own words, describe what 'contingency arrangements' means.

_____

_____

_____

_____

_____

10. List the three different types of microphones that could be available to presenters at a conference and their particular advantages.

_____

_____

_____

_____

11. What contingency plans should be in place to ensure the security of any large amounts of cash that are accumulated during the registration period?

_____

_____

_____

_____

_____

_____

_____

_____

12. List 10 of the many duties of a chairperson or moderator at a conference.

_____

_____

_____

_____

_____

_____

_____

_____

_____

_____

_____

_____

_____

_____

_____

5 Follow up conference proceedings

This final element considers the various outcomes of the conference and how they may be recorded and/or reported. This includes financial reports and reports based on feedback and observations.

Next, the text explains the process of preparing conference papers for publication and distribution, then the writing and dispatch of post-conference correspondence, and finally, the settlement of any outstanding financial matters and records.

5.1 Conference outcomes are recorded, reported and/or followed up

The conference outcomes could include a wide range of results, both measurable and intangible. These could be flow-on effects on the company's business, such as a heightened profile in the marketplace or an increase in sales of the company's products, improved staff performance, enthusiasm, and commitment to tasks.

Conference reports

Written reports prepared by the conference committee and the convener for the organisation's board of directors would provide an overview of the tangible results of the conference as well as considering whether the purposes and required outcomes were met adequately.

Financial report

Depending on organisational requirements, the first document produced may be a financial report showing income generated from fees, sponsorships and the exhibition (if one was arranged) against the total cost of organising the conference, and the outcome as to whether a profit or loss situation resulted. This outcome would need to be compared against the original budget provided by the financial controller of the company.

A more detailed analysis, if required, would compare the previous conference costs and income, item by item, with the current conference costs and income generated.

Sessions overview and general management reports

Other reports could contain an overview of the sessions, the number of attendees, and whether this fluctuated over the days of the conference. In particular, the popularity of different topics or speakers could be assessed based on the number of attendees at each session.

The performance of staff and helpers may also be rated or commented on and the methods used for registration, room set-ups and managing the movement of delegates to the various session rooms examined, if there was dissatisfaction with this aspect of the conference.

Other sections of the report(s) would consider the suitability of the venue for future conferences and other details such as whether the equipment hire and catering arrangements were satisfactory. If an exhibition or trade fair had been arranged, with or without sponsorships, this too would be the subject of examination for satisfaction levels on all sides.

Overview of pre-conference activities

Other important aspects could be addressed in the reports, such as:

- Was the budget realistic?
- Was it too generous or too restricted?
- How satisfactory was the promotional campaign?

- Did it generate many more delegates than were originally expected to attend?
- How beneficial was the web page in encouraging people to register and how frequently was the online registration form used?
- Were the brochures and mail-shots attractive and well-received?
- Was the timing of the mailing(s) correct?
- If a professional publicist was used, were they worth their fee? Did they bring fresh, effective ideas to the promotion?
- If a computerised registration system was used, was it satisfactory? Did it save time?
- Did registration procedures on the first day of the conference run smoothly?
- Would we do it all the same way again?
- Are there things we would do differently next time?
- What could we change and why?

Evaluation questionnaires

An analysis of the evaluation questionnaires completed by delegates could also prove to be enlightening as to how attendees viewed the conference:

- If it satisfied their expectations or needs.
- If the program was balanced.
- How they rated the speakers—their knowledge and performances.
- If they learnt anything valuable, or felt it was worthwhile in terms of money or time expended.
- Was the social program enjoyable?
- Were the costs appropriate?
- Was the catering satisfactory, below average or good?
- Was the venue suitable?
- What aspects of the conference would they have changed?

Feedback from sponsors and exhibitors

Another important section of the reports would focus on feedback gained from the sponsors and exhibitors. For example, were they satisfied with the results they achieved from the conference, and was the space suitable? What would they change about it or the management of the conference? How could it be improved in the future? Would they exhibit at or sponsor another conference by your company? Why or why not?

Follow-up

If constructive suggestions were made about changes that could be implemented at future conferences, these should be recorded in the reports for further discussion and consideration by management or future conference committees when planning and arranging the next conference.

If a profit was not one of the achievements of the conference, though one may have been expected, an assessment should be made as to whether the outlay was, nevertheless, considered to be worthwhile for the organisation in terms of its future growth and standing among its peers.

5.2 Conference papers are prepared for publication and distributed within designated timelines

Even though the conference is over, there are still tasks to be completed. One of these is the publication of the proceedings. To do this, copies of the full text of papers presented by speakers and keynote speakers need to be compiled in the order in which they were given. If there was an opening address by a special guest or plenary session speakers, these talks should be included.

Format of the proceedings

The proceedings are usually presented in a normal book format—perhaps A4 size or smaller—with a title page, contents list, an acknowledgements page and perhaps an introduction written by the conference convener. This last could be personal reflections on the conference and an overview or perhaps a summing up of its content, or a more formal introduction to the material that follows. How elaborate the proceedings book will be will depend entirely on the conference committee's directions and the budget. There are no hard-and-fast rules as far as presentation is concerned.

Editing the text

It may be decided to include only excerpts from the addresses given by speakers rather than the whole text, so an editor would need to be employed to read and shorten the presentations as necessary. Again, it is the personal choice of the convener or the committee members—but if the organisation has set down certain procedures or requirements in this respect, these will obviously be followed.

Other content

If some positive or enthusiastic remarks were made by delegates on their evaluation forms, or in person to conference organisers, these could perhaps be gathered together for an opening page preceding the body of the book containing the papers.

At the beginning of each entry, a brief resumé or biography of the presenter could open the page, perhaps with the inclusion of a photograph provided by the person, or an informal photograph taken during the session. These sorts of added extras can place a conference in context and give an idea or reminder of the atmosphere and environment to the reader.

The proceedings would also include a list of delegates' names and a list of sponsors. If an exhibition was set up, a list of participating companies may be included at the discretion of the conference committee.

Tape-recording some sessions

Depending on the formal or informal nature of the conference, some presenters may have spoken without notes or off-the-cuff in question-and-answer sessions. In these circumstances, the session would hopefully have been tape-recorded. The tape would need to be transcribed and then edited down to the essence of the message the speaker or group was trying to convey, or the topics discussed. A summary of these types of sessions would be sufficient, with key messages included.

It can sometimes be helpful to record the keynote speakers' addresses as, generally speaking, these would be reproduced in full in the proceedings document. This would be particularly important if the speaker has not provided a copy of their speech or has spoken from brief notes.

Alternative media

A CD-ROM of the proceedings could also be made in both HTML and PDF formats for those that require it, and depending on how much demand there would be for such a production. The disk could also include the final version of the conference web site as well as the list of attendees and sponsors.

Depending on the organisation's policy, a complementary copy of the proceedings may be sent to all members; alternatively it would go to those who have previously requested and paid for a copy. Sponsors and delegates may also be sent copies. Additional copies could be produced for sale, if this were considered to be appropriate by the committee.

5.3 Post-conference correspondence is prepared and dispatched within designated timelines

Letters of thanks will need to be written promptly after the conference—within the following week or so—and sent to all those who made significant contributions to the organisation, management or quality of the conference.

In particular, letters should be sent to all speakers, guest speakers and those who chaired or moderated each of the sessions. Thank those concerned for their time and the effort they put into their contributions. If fees had been agreed on for some presenters, and their fees have not been paid earlier, then a cheque should be enclosed with the letter of thanks.

Special thank-you letters should also be sent to sponsors who contributed to the financial viability of the conference or provided different items to enhance the quality of the experience for delegates. Exhibitors should also be thanked for their presence and for providing another facet to the conference, making it more interesting and attractive for delegates.

5.4 Receipts and payments are finalised and conference funds acquitted in accordance with organisational procedures and audit requirements

All receipts for registration fees and payments for any social activities should have been distributed before or at the conference. Most payments for services provided such as equipment hire, catering, venue hire and so on should be settled promptly, or the invoices passed on to the relevant department of the organisation if they have not already been paid.

Once any outstanding invoices have been settled, it would be the responsibility of the financial controller or accountant of the organisation to ensure that all the financial records compiled during the conference are appropriately recorded according to the company's procedural and auditing protocols.

EXERCISE 10

1. What do you think 'intangible' means?

_____

_____

2. Give three examples of intangible, positive outcomes that could arise as a result of a company arranging a conference.

_____

_____

_____

_____

_____

_____

_____

_____

_____

_____

3. What could provide tangible results of the conference? Name two things.

_____

_____

_____

_____

4. Name one way you could gauge the popularity of different topics or speakers at a conference.

_____

_____

_____

_____

5. What would be another method of finding out how delegates viewed the conference and whether they enjoyed it or found it valuable?

_____

_____

_____

_____

_____

6. What comprises the 'proceedings' of a conference?

_____

_____

_____

_____

7. Why might an editor be needed to work on the proceedings of the conference?

_____

_____

_____

_____

_____

8. What two things should be included at the end of the proceedings?

_____

_____

_____

_____

9. For what reasons would you tape-record some presentations or speakers?

_____

_____

_____

_____

_____

_____

10. Who would be ultimately responsible for recording the financial costs of and revenue generated by the conference?

_____

_____

SKILLS TEST

1. Research an aspect of legislation that would affect the planning and management of a conference. For example, Occupational Health and Safety and environmental issues, anti-discrimination or industrial relations. Write a few paragraphs about the legislation and why it was introduced, or what effect it is intended to have. Then prepare a short talk and present it to your group or class.

2. ROLE PLAY—working with a partner.

You have been selected to make the arrangements for your small company's annual staff conference to be held in the Hunter Valley, north of Sydney on September 7 and 8. There will be 60 attendees.

First, create a title and theme for the conference—it is your choice.

The sessions will be as follows:

> DAY 1: 9am Plenary session—keynote speaker; 10.15am Sales Director—review of year; 11.15am Morning tea; 11.30am New products (PowerPoint presentation); 12.45pm Lunch; 2pm New products continues (PowerPoint presentation); 3.30pm Afternoon tea; 4pm Changes in work practices technology—General Manager; 7.30pm Conference dinner—guest speaker.

> DAY 2: 9–11am Discussion groups on three different topics for delegates to choose from—Sessions A, B or C, to be held in separate syndicate rooms (a moderator will be needed for each group). After morning tea, a plenary session will be addressed by the Financial Controller, between 11.30am and 12.45pm. 2pm Panel discussion with all presenters, followed by a question-and-answer session, to be moderated by the Publications Director. Following afternoon tea, at 4pm a plenary session will be addressed by the Chief Executive.

To clarify what you would need to do next, draw up a draft program or simple timetable for the conference to use as a working tool. (This will make the organisation phase easier to manage.) Include tea breaks and lunch periods in the timetable. Then, using the following requirements for the conference, write a detailed checklist of all the arrangements you will need to make.

Conference requirements: an appropriate venue; a suitable keynote speaker, guest speaker and presenters; equipment for the PowerPoint presentations; microphones; catering; accommodation for all delegates and the keynote and guest speakers overnight.

PLAN AND MANAGE CONFERENCES © BEVERLEY L. WEYNTON

Because the company's budget for the conference is quite generous, you can afford to employ a conference manager to assist you in these tasks. Select a partner to act as the conference manager and brief them on the arrangements you need to make. Take your draft program and checklist of requirements to the meeting.

Your partner, as the conference manager, should question you on all the details. Discuss and negotiate an appropriate fee, the type of speakers available and their fees, equipment hire, catering and all the other details described above. The conference manager may be able to make further suggestions about how you might enhance the conference or make it more exciting for delegates— perhaps an excursion or some team-building activities.

Before you begin, it would be advisable for you and your partner to re-read the sections in the text about making conference arrangements such as units 1.2 *Conference facilities requirements..*, 1.3 *Speakers are identified..*, 1.4 *Conference program is drafted..*, 3.1 *Conference arrangements are made..*, 3.3 *Participants' special needs...* Make some notes so you are both prepared for the discussion and to make sure you will attend to all the required details. Try to make this exercise as realistic as possible.

Draw up a complete program and then report back to your group or the class and explain the arrangements you have made.

3. PROBLEM SOLVING

Think about a possible major problem that could arise to disrupt the conference. For example, speakers failing to arrive, venue disabled by a power disruption. Prepare a contingency plan to meet such a problem and describe how you would implement it.

4. You have been given the task of writing **formal** thank-you letters to the speakers who made presentations and to the moderators of the sessions at a conference your company has held. Using the information in **Element 5–5.3** as a guide, prepare letters of thanks for the guest speaker and a moderator.

5. On behalf of the conference committee, write an **informal** letter of thanks which will be sent to several work colleagues who helped with the set-ups of the session rooms at your company's recent conference.

6. Working in a small group, read through *Preparation of evaluation questionnaire* in 1.7 *Administration requirements...* on page 40. Then, based on some of the ideas presented there, draw up a questionnaire for delegates to complete after the conclusion of a conference organised by the conference committee of a large association or professional body.

Before you begin designing the layout of the questionnaire and writing the questions, decide how you want delegates to respond—with a rating system 1–5; by ticking or circling one of several options provided on the form or by making written responses. You may decide to use all three methods or only one. You may also like to identify the type of association that requires this information so you can make the questions appropriate.

7. Exchange your questionnaire with other groups and compare and discuss them. Consider whether any other elements or questions could have been included and whether the information requested in the questionnaire would be helpful to future conference planning committees.